Immigrants of the Kingdom of God

Immigrants of the Kingdom of God

*Reflections on Immigration
as a Metaphor of Christian Discipleship*

ANNANG ASUMANG

WIPF & STOCK · Eugene, Oregon

IMMIGRANTS OF THE KINGDOM OF GOD
Reflections on Immigration as a Metaphor of Christian Discipleship

Copyright © 2008 Annang Asumang. All rights reserved. Except for brief quotations in critical publications or reviews, no part of this book may be reproduced in any manner without prior written permission from the publisher. Write: Permissions, Wipf and Stock Publishers, 199 W. 8th Ave., Suite 3, Eugene, OR 97401.

www.wipfandstock.com

ISBN: 978-1-55635-829-6

Manufactured in the U.S.A.

Unless otherwise stated, scripture quotations are from the New International Version of the Bible, made available by the International Bible Society Copyright © 1973, 1978, 1984 and accessed online at http://www.ibs.org/niv/index.php. All rights reserved throughout the world. Used by permission of International Bible Society.

Contents

Preface vii

Introduction: Immigration and the Kingdom of God: Yesterday and Today 1

Abraham: Father of Immigrants and Friend of God: Looking for the Heavenly City 10

Joseph: You Intended to Harm Me but God Intended it for Good: Turning Your Bitter Experiences into Good 21

Israel: Let My People Go So They Will Worship Me in the Desert: Experiencing God's Power in Life's Wilderness 34

Samson: How Can You Be Tied Up and Subdued: Why Some Immigrants Fail 48

Ruth: Your People Will Be My People: Integrating Successfully in a Foreign Land 63

Jesus: The Word Became Flesh and Dwelt Among Us: God the Immigrant 79

Paul, Barnabas, Stephen and Apollos: These People, Who Have Turned the World Upside Down, Have Come Here Also: Christianity was Largely Spread by Immigrants 92

Final Thoughts: Immigration and the Future of Christianity in the West 111

Preface

THE CURRENT INTERNATIONAL DEBATE on immigration has largely ignored one of its most important elements. This has to do with the effect of immigration on religion. In this instance, we are concerned with Christianity and immigration. From the perspective of the average Christian, some burning questions have not been adequately debated. What should be the attitude of the Christian to the immigrant? In what particular ways should local churches respond to the social challenges that immigrants bring to their communities? How should the Christian immigrant interpret his or her own experiences in a foreign environment? More pointedly, how does God view immigration? What does the Bible really say about the phenomenon?

It is admitted that we are living in an era that is far removed from the biblical times. The organization of nation states and their borders are far too sophisticated to demand a return to practices of a pre-scientific era. In addition, the major factors that are fuelling the modern trends of immigration are completely different from those of first century Palestine. These caveats notwithstanding, Christians have no choice but to allow God's word to shape the way they answer contemporary questions. This means that practically, it is only as believers take the attitude of the Bible to immigration seriously that they can make God-honoring contributions to the debate.

This book is a biblical reflection on one of this decade's most important social and international concerns. Its main objective is not to examine the sociological phenomenon or the political and economic implications of immigration. Inevitably, the conclusions from this study should inform how we approach immigration as a socio-economic subject. Given that I have no major competencies in this area of the topic, I have avoided in-depth analysis of the socio-political implications of immigration. What is lacking in that area is however made up for by attending to the Bible's teaching on the subject.

Preface

This attitude of the Bible to immigration is not presented in a systematic and straightforward manner. It is largely presented through stories. Consequently, this study has not approached the Bible in an organized question and answers fashion. Rather, by examining the individual experiences of some of the giants of the Bible, we will discover insights that should shape our attitude to immigration. Such an approach has the added advantage of not prejudging the answers.

In approaching each story of immigration in the Bible, I have adopted a two-tier system of interpretation. Each of the stories is examined from the point of view of the phenomenon of immigration itself. In addition however, the story's depiction of Christian discipleship that challenges all believers will also be emphasized. Such a method, I hope, will make this study valuable to both Christian immigrants and non-immigrants alike. Ultimately, all Christians are aliens of the kingdom of God and immigrants in this world.

The reflections may be studied by individual Christians for their own edification. However, throughout the book, the emphasis is on application within a communal setting. Accordingly, the chapters will also prove useful as bases for group bible studies. To help in these discussions, brief questions are provided at the end of each chapter. These may be improved and used as starting points for further reflections.

It remains for me, at this stage, to express my sincere thanks and heartfelt gratitude to all those who have inspired and encouraged me during the preparation. To start with, my deepest gratitude goes to Dr Raymond Akwayena for his constant challenge and encouragement. He has helpfully critiqued and corrected many parts of this book. Thanks also to Jacob Mensah whose comments on some of the draft chapters were extremely helpful. Dr Elijah Paintsil, with whom a brief conversation over a year ago inspired the basic idea of the book, deserves recognition. I am also grateful to my wife, Edna, whose capacity for endurance never fails to amaze me.

Introduction

Immigration and the Kingdom of God: Yesterday and Today

THE ISSUE OF IMMIGRATION has assumed a very high profile in the mass media, academia and politics in recent years. Historically, it has always been an important social, political and economic matter, relevant to governments and their citizens alike. This decade has however seen an increasingly heated and sometimes overheated debate about the benefits and disadvantages of immigration. With the world seemingly shrinking through technological advancement, massive movement of people and goods across borders should be expected. Yet, the scale of the movement and its potential consequences appear to have taken most countries by surprise.

The factors fuelling increased immigration in the present decade are not difficult to identify. The vast differences in economic growth and the gap in the social and political progress between the developed and underdeveloped countries are the major factors. These, coupled with political instability and civil wars in some parts of the world have resulted in the substantial movement of economic migrants. The sad reality is that, for many young adults in less developed countries, immigration has become a necessity.

On the other hand, recipient countries have often, and understandably, felt destabilized and perhaps even frightened about the possible consequences of immigration. In many of these countries, the concern has been the possible negative effects on the economy, demography and culture. In the last few years for example, the large influx of immigrants from Mexico and Latin American countries into North America has prompted an acrimonious argument in the US. The passionate debate and subsequent failure of the Comprehensive Immigration Reform Bill in the

US Congress during 2006/07 only serve to illustrate the strong emotions that such issues ignite. In the end, the President's own Republican Party refused to back his plans to grant amnesty to twelve million resident illegal immigrants.

In Europe, the situation has also been brought to the fore by the expansion of the European Union to include former communist countries. Citizens from the poorer parts of Europe are now free to travel to the richer countries for work, education and leisure. These immigrants no doubt provide cheaper sources of labor for the host countries. Their presence has however resulted in the perceived displacement of indigenous people from their employment and led to resentment.

In France, Germany, United Kingdom and other major European countries, there is an ongoing soul-searching on what should be the appropriate policies towards immigrants. Similar debates are underway in Canada, Russia, Japan and Australia. Moderately rich countries such as South Africa, South Korea, Malaysia, Argentina and Brazil are also involved in equivalent national discussions. Immigration is clearly a worldwide socio-political hot potato.

What has not been adequately discussed during these debates is the influence of immigration on religion in the host countries. Though the increase in the number of Moslem immigrants in the West has been raised in some publications, there has not been any significant analysis of the impact of immigration on the Christian faith. This issue is important because there is evidence to suggest that in the last few years, a renewed movement of God among the Churches of the industrialized countries is occurring. Increased church attendances and reversal of the fortunes of some of the Christian Churches in the Western democracies are being reported in several ecclesiastical censuses. Does immigration have anything to do with this "spiritual renewal"?

The English Church Census, conducted by the independent Christian Research Organization in 2005, for example, showed that the decades of dwindling church membership and growth in the United Kingdom has been stemmed. Today, some of the churches in London are being filled to capacity with vibrant young people who are excited about their faith in the Lord Jesus. This was not the case ten years ago when the same churches were lethargic, half-empty and facing extinction. Similarly, in some of the major cities of the UK, a spiritual renewal appears to be under

Introduction

way. Several churches in the provinces have been enlivened with people worshipping Christ with confidence and pride.

One of the reasons for this apparent transformation is immigration. A recent survey has shown for example, that whereas people of African and Caribbean origins make up two percent of the UK's population, they account for more than two-thirds of Sunday churchgoers in London. Similarly, the largest independent church in UK today, which sees twelve thousand people attending a church service each Sunday, was planted and is pastored by a Nigerian immigrant. The *Hillsong Church*, one other fast growing church in London that attracts a total of more than ten thousand attendances at its services, was started by Australian immigrants.

Since the recent immigration of many Polish, Latvian and Croatian citizens to other regions of the continent, the Roman Catholic Church in Europe is also experiencing revitalization. Several congregations of the London dioceses of the Roman Catholic Church now require a number of sessions of Sunday services to cater for the increasing numbers of immigrants from Europe and South America. The Church of England is equally experiencing a fresh awakening in some of its congregations. It is significant that despite its depressing state, two senior clergymen of that denomination who are making some impact and seeking to restore a truly prophetic voice to the Anglican Church are Archbishop John Sentamu of York and Bishop Nazir-Ali of Rochester. Both are immigrants.

Similar trends seem to be occurring in other countries of the West. For example, in Kiev, the capital of erstwhile communist Ukraine, twenty five thousand vibrant worshippers of the *Embassy of God* Church, led by Pastor Sunday Adelaja, a Nigerian immigrant, fill a Sports Hall each Sunday to hear the gospel of Christ. This church's influence has extended far into the very corridors of political power in that fledging democracy. In Amsterdam, Rev. Stanley Hofwijks, an immigrant from Suriname, pastors the eighteen hundred member *Maranatha Ministries* whose services are crammed with energetic worshippers hungry to meet the Spirit of God at work among His people.

In largely Catholic France and Germany, the trends are not as dramatic. The secularization of these dominant European powers remains entrenched. Yet, even here, there are perceptible signs of change. For instance, over the last three decades, there has been a fourfold increase in the number of Evangelical Churches in France. Fifty percent of this increase is due to immigrants. Recent reports of increased church attendances in the Catholic Churches of France have also been attributed in part to immigrants from Europe, Africa and South America. The same is also true of Germany. The simple fact is the future of Christianity in several European countries is increasingly becoming dependent on immigrants.

It must be admitted that the presence of immigrants alone does not explain the transformation of fortunes of western churches. Other factors such as the general sense of spiritual emptiness, popularization of charismatic forms of worship and renewed interest among the population in the message of the Bible has contributed to the trend. Nevertheless, it is noteworthy that a significant proportion of the people who appear to respond most to these awakenings are immigrants.

The situation in the US is also interesting. Over the last thirty years, it has been reported that church attendance in the US has remained static at thirty to forty percent of the population. On the surface, this "stagnation" may appear different from what is happening elsewhere in the world. However, when examined in detail, it emerges that there is a massive decline in attendance in some of the churches in the country that is being offset by an equally substantial increase in other congregations and denominations.

For example, within the traditional mainline denominations who had been suffering decline in membership, such as the Presbyterian and United Methodist Churches, the fastest growing congregations are among Korean immigrants. During the last twenty years, three thousand, five hundred new Korean immigrant Presbyterian and Methodist congregations have been established in the US.

Equally, total attendance at Roman Catholic Church services in America has remained steady and perhaps growing, due to the increased number of immigrants from the Latin American countries. The fastest growing churches in the US are the independent churches, many of which have significant proportion of new immigrants. Immigration is consistently playing a pivotal role in the trend of worldwide regeneration of Christian congregations. This effect of immigration on religion however, is not a new phenomenon.

IMMIGRATION IN THE BIBLE

Immigration has always had this transforming effect on societies since the dawn of history. Throughout biblical times, God has used immigration

Introduction

and immigrants in significant ways to spread His kingdom and transform societies. Many of these change agents were real immigrants who had been displaced from one region and culture to another. Others were immigrants in the figurative sense. For, it is evident that God's Kingdom cannot be spread except by people who know in their inner beings what it means to be in the world but not be part of it. God requires all those who want to be light in this dark world and salt in a tasteless and decaying environment to learn how to live as immigrants, aliens and ambassadors for Christ.

The influence of immigration on the recent renewal of western churches is therefore not a new phenomenon. Indeed, the rapid growth of the early Church in the first and second centuries was largely due to the immigration of Jews throughout the Roman Empire. According to John Elliot, distinguished Professor Emeritus of Theology in University of San Francisco, "the attraction of educational opportunities (such as the university at Tarsus) and health spas (at the renowned Asclespian spring shrines) and athletic and dramatic festivals, religious pilgrimages, mass movements of deported groups, the banishment of individuals, and the peregrinations of assorted itinerant philosophers and missionaries" ensured a massive flow of migrant workers and families throughout the empire[1]. Jewish immigrant settlements in Egypt, Antioch, Italy, Ephesus, and the whole of Asia Minor became the hotbed of Christian activity from which the Word of God spread to the "uttermost parts of the world".

One typical illustration of the influence of immigrants in early Christianity is found in the commissioning of Paul and Barnabas for the Gentile mission at the Church of Antioch in Acts 13. Luke names several prophets and teachers in this congregation—Barnabas, Simeon (nicknamed Niger), Lucius of Cyrene, Manaen and Saul. It is not accidental that each one of these spiritual leaders was an immigrant from a different country. Barnabas was a Jew who was born in Cyprus where he owned a land (Acts 4:36–37). Simeon's nickname, Niger, suggests that he was a black man, Lucius came from Cyrene in North Africa, and Manaen was an educated aristocrat from Rome. These immigrants in Antioch, together of course with Paul, a Jew who grew up as an immigrant in Tarsus, formed the core ministry of the thriving church in Antioch. And it was from here

---

1. John H Elliot, *A Home for the Homeless: A Sociological Exegesis of 1 Peter: Its Situation and Strategy* Philadelphia, Fortress 1981:67.

that a deliberate effort was made, led by the Spirit of God, to evangelize the world.

This pattern was repeated in other parts of the Roman Empire. Immigrants, especially Jewish immigrants, were at the center of the spread of the Christian religion from its inception. Having experienced the power of God on the day of Pentecost, the Jewish immigrants on pilgrimage to Jerusalem (Acts 2:9–11) dispersed to all the regions of the empire to spread the gospel. These people knew what exactly it meant to be living in the Roman Empire and yet to belong to another domain which is that of the Kingdom of Christ. God was therefore glad to use them for His programme of transforming His world.

According to Prof Elliot again, Jewish immigrants were sometimes "excluded from voting and landholding privileges as well as from the chief civic offices and honors, they enjoyed only limited legal protection while ... they still shared full responsibilities with the citizenry for all financial burdens, such as tributes, taxes, and production quotas"[2]. For those of them who became Christians, such an experience prepared them to be Christ's ambassadors. They knew on a daily basis that though they lived in the Roman Empire, they were treated and regarded as people who were different.

When the earliest Christians described discipleship to the Lord Jesus with terms that depicted them as aliens, foreigners, sojourners and strangers in the world, they had practically experienced life as foreigners already. It was not at all difficult for them to understand Paul's statement that their "citizenship is in heaven" (Phil 3:20). In their daily lives, they experienced life as if they were citizens of another domain, as foreigners and immigrants. An interesting quote from an anonymous letter, which was written in the second or third century AD, summarizes how the earliest believers understood their identity:

> "For Christians cannot be distinguished from the rest of the human race by country or language or customs. They do not live in cities of their own; they do not use a peculiar form of speech; they do not follow an eccentric manner of life ... Yet, although they live in Greek and barbarian cities alike, as each man's lot has been cast, and follow the customs of the country in clothing and food and other matters of daily living, at the same time they give proof of

---

2. John Elliot, *1 Peter: A New Translation with Introduction and Commentary*, New York, Doubleday, 2000:94.

Introduction

the remarkable and admittedly extraordinary constitution of their own commonwealth. They live in their own countries, but only as aliens. They have a share in everything as citizens, and endure everything as foreigners.[3]

The Christian condition is therefore an immigrant condition, both in real terms, and metaphorically. If only Christians lived by this mindset, they will make a remarkable difference to the communities in which God has placed them. If, on the other hand, they choose not to bind their hearts and minds to the government of God but rather live by earthly standards, their societies will be stumbling. Our investigation of the phenomenon of immigration in the Bible is therefore a very crucial project. For, through our study, we shall come to insightful answers on how believers must live in this world as Christ's ambassadors.

In this book we wish to focus on immigration in the Bible. What does the Bible actually say about immigration? What role did immigrants play in the spread of God's Kingdom? What conclusions can we draw from the Bible to help us answer the questions that nations, Churches and individuals are facing today with regard to immigration? How should an immigrant interpret his experiences?

There are several different ways that one may choose to investigate this subject. The method of approach we have chosen is to examine the lives of the giants of the Bible. On doing so, even in a cursory manner, we are immediately confronted with the undeniable reality that most, if not all the spiritual giants of the Bible, were immigrants, and aliens in their environment. Some, like Abraham, Ruth, Esther or Daniel were complete strangers where they were. Others like Moses, David or Paul had at some stage of their lives been strangers and immigrants, prepared and trained by God before being re-inserted into their societies. It is evident that they had to be different to be used by God. We shall discover that one important aspect of their "differentness" was their immigration status.

Abraham was called by God to leave his country, his secure business and family, and to follow God's leadership as an immigrant and ambassador of God's blessings. Joseph on the other hand, through a series of "accidents", found himself living as a migrant worker, a house slave in particular, in a foreign land. He must have said to himself on thousands

---

3. *The Letter to Diognetus:* Quoted from Cyril Richardson, ed., *Early Christian Fathers*, Philadelphia, Westminster Press 1953: 217-18.

of occasions; "it was not [them] who sent me here, but God" (Gen 45:8). In learning to interpret his experiences from God's perspective, Joseph turned calamity for himself, his master, his host country and his own people into success and glory.

The most profound and detailed story of immigration in the Bible is that of the people of Israel. While they suffered under the cruel tyranny of the Egyptians, God heard their cry for deliverance and in His own time, delivered them. Their forty years of wilderness travel was however, a mixture of the positive and the negative. There, they experienced both the power and presence of God to prepare them as His people. During the same time they experienced periods of intense testing of their faith. All immigrants, real or metaphorical, share this experience of testing and preparation with the people of Israel in the wilderness.

The Old Testament also describes the exploits of migrant women such as Sarah, Rahab, Ruth and Esther, to name but a few. These migrant women brought tremendous blessings to generations after them through their persistence and faithfulness. Ruth was the typical Gentile, who rejected her roots in order to follow Jehovah and share the heritage of God's people. Esther may have thought she was in an impossible situation in exile. That is, until God's time came, when she realized that she had been placed where she was at that particular time for a specific purpose in keeping with Jehovah's kingdom.

Not all immigrants in the Bible were successful in their mission. Some like Samson and Lot lost their focus, became self indulgent, and ceased to be light in the world of darkness. Samson in particular was a wasted opportunity. He lacked self-restraint and discipline. He was a gambler who enjoyed the thrills of near escapes. Samson is a good example of how to fail as an immigrant.

Few people appreciate that the Bible describes Jesus as a Foreigner and an Alien in this world. In Him, God became an immigrant in the world He had created, and through Him, reconciled humanity to Himself. As a baby, Jesus became a refugee and an asylum seeker in Egypt, fleeing from the swords of Herod's soldiers. And in His ministry, he was homeless, living like a fox that has no hole to sleep in, a Son of man with nowhere to lay His head. Yet, the Lord Jesus knew His mission as God's Agent, sent to draw people and reconcile them to His Father.

Not only Jesus, but also Paul, Stephen, Barnabas, Apollos, John, Peter—the major "movers and shakers" of the New Testament, were at

Introduction

one time or the other immigrants and foreigners. Stephen's development as a Hellenistic Jew in the Diaspora, Philip's Greek background, Barnabas' development in Cyprus, Paul's birth and training in Tarsus and Apollos' schooling as a Jew in Egypt prepared them to become the mighty men of God. It was through the ministry of these immigrants that the whole world was turned upside down for Christ. This fact certainly has very crucial lessons to contribute to the debate on immigration and religion.

In the following chapters, we shall examine the lives of some of these immigrants of the Bible more closely. This will help us to form a view on how to respond to the various issues raised by the present international debate on immigration.

We shall also discover how God uses the life of the immigrant as a metaphor of Christian discipleship. The immigrant's displacement, rootlessness, marginalization, double personality, and liminality resonate very well with the nature of discipleship to the Lord Jesus Christ. All believers are called to be aliens of the Kingdom of God and ambassadors of Christ the King. Like the immigrants of the Bible, believers are also called to follow Christ and be His ministers of grace so that through them His promised Kingdom will come.

DISCUSSION QUESTIONS

1. The word "discipleship" means different things to different believers. Generally however, it describes how Christians understand and define themselves—it is the believer's understanding of his or her identity. Can you list and explain some of the various ways that the New Testament depicts the identity of a Christian?

2. It could be argued that by defining immigration as a parable or metaphor of Christian discipleship, one is legitimizing the phenomenon of immigration. What do you think about this argument?

3. What do you think are some of the reasons why some immigrants in developed countries are very religious?

Abraham

Father of Immigrants and Friend of God:
Looking for the Heavenly City

THE VAST REPUTATION OF Abraham in the three major religions of the world underlines his historical significance. In the Bible, Abraham was the most senior among the patriarchs who demonstrated how human beings, even after the fall of Adam, may yet walk in close friendship with God. Other faithful men before him, like Enoch and Noah, had distinguished themselves by their faith and been recipients of God's covenants. Yet, it was Abraham who begun the trend of living consistently in such a way as to reverse the curse of Adam. Indeed, God later introduced Himself to Moses as, "the God of Abraham". To put it in modern terminology, God re-branded Himself with "the Abrahamic trademark"! It is no wonder therefore that Abraham soars in reputation above many of the men of God in the Bible.

What is particularly remarkable is that Abraham acquired this towering reputation through immigration. In his assessment of the patriarch, the author of the Book of Hebrews records that Abraham received God's approval because he lived by faith and obedience, "like a stranger in a foreign country . . . looking forward to the city with foundations" (Heb 11:8–10). In other words, Abraham's immigration status was a major factor that contributed to his impressive reputation.

We do well therefore to examine what the Bible means by living "like stranger in a foreign country . . . looking forward to the city with foundation". For, these features of Abraham's life are linked together and describe the nature of Christian discipleship. God calls upon believers to live like strangers in a foreign country, look for the heavenly city, and do so by faith and obedience.

Abraham

LOOKING FOR THE HEAVENLY CITY

To understand what is meant by "looking for a city with foundations" we need to go back to Genesis, to the very beginning of human existence. For, Abraham was not the first immigrant in the Bible. Adam became the first immigrant when he was banished from God's presence. Adam was displaced from the place of perfect communion with his Creator as a result of his sin. And consequently, all of Adam's descendants have inherited this human condition. When Cain murdered his brother, he also became "a restless wanderer on the earth" (Gen 4:12). Cain, like his father, became a vagabond and an asylum seeker. The theme of immigration therefore goes far back to the beginning of human existence.

What is most noteworthy about Cain's immigration is that he did not just wander from God's presence. The Bible tells us that unlike his father, Cain institutionalized his separation from the Garden of Eden by building a city for himself (Gen 4:17). This action was momentous, not only because it is the first mention of a city in the Bible. It was momentous because it describes the very ethos and quest of Cain's life. For, unlike the modern era, an ancient city represented its citizen's vision and ideals. To say one belonged to a particular city meant one was committed to a particular mindset, culture and social vision. A city in the Bible was symbolic of the type of social vision and lifestyle that one had chosen.

It was for this reason that the Garden of Eden was also described as the city of God. For that was where the law of God reigned in perfection. Once defiled by man's disobedience and faithlessness, that place was barred to humanity. Centuries later, God chose Jerusalem as an earthly symbol of His heavenly city (Ps 50:2). And just as the world begun with the city of God, it will also end with the city of God (Rev 21: 1–2). Similarly, when Jesus spoke of the kingdom of God or the kingdom of heaven, He was also referring to this "city" where people live in perfect obedience to God.

Unlike the Garden of Eden, Cain's city was built with a different ethos and philosophy. The Bible tells us that Cain's city was named after his son. In so doing, he established and formalized his total rejection of God and His set of rules. Cain built a city to rival the Garden of Eden. His city was built upon the foundations of rebellion against Jehovah, and in competition with God's system of regulations.

When civilizations reject God's rule, teach their children that God does not exist and enact laws that are in direct opposition to the Word of God, they are, like Cain, setting up a rival city in opposition to God's City. They are doing exactly what Cain did. Cain looked for a city whose architect and builder was human—human abilities, human power, human desires, human glory, and human hope. Abraham on the other hand, looked for a different city whose architect and builder was God. Cain's life was not of faith and obedience to God. Abraham's life was of faith and obedience. Not all immigrants share in Abraham's inheritance. Some share in the inheritance of Cain.

After Cain, the next major incident in the Bible that involved the building of a city is recorded in Gen 11. There, we are told that as people continued to migrate, they decided to build themselves a city, "with a tower that reaches to the heavens, so that we may make a name for ourselves" (Gen 11: 4). Having rejected the city of God, these immigrants openly declared their complete rebellion by attempting to build a city whose citadel rose up into the heavens. They reasoned, "We have got to beat God in this. We have got to show that Eden is not good enough. We have got to make a name for ourselves in opposition to God's laws. Now that we have rejected God's rule, let us show Him what we can do".

A lot of people speak and think like that in today's world. In several homes, universities, offices and even churches, the Word of God is ridiculed, and rejected in similar fashion to what the people of Babel did. In civil society today, there are men and women who openly defy God to His face. To such people, God may as well be deaf or dumb or even dead. Such people are building a defiant "city" like the people of Babel. Like the men of Shinar, they are literally poking at God's nose.

It was in the centre of this spiritual rebellion at Babel, that God commanded Abraham, "Leave your country, your people and your father's household and go to the land I will show you" (Gen 12:1). In other words, God called Abraham to repudiate the ideology of Babel and migrate to "the land" of God's vision. Abraham rejected the ideology of Shinar to look for the city with true foundations.

How bold this man was to reject the haughtiness of his contemporaries. He chose to live differently and to seek life in obedience to God. Abraham committed himself to live like a stranger whose ethos and ideals were locked into a different set of dreams. He rejected the creeds and agenda set up by his generation to look for a different agenda. Abraham moved in a different direction from his contemporaries.

Abraham

Looking for an idealized "land" is a characteristic feature of the immigrant life. Sociologists point out that one defining characteristic of the immigrant is that he is constantly conscious of a "homeland" far away. The immigrant has considerable emotional and psychological attachment to this homeland. And this consciousness significantly affects his behavior in the host country. He may struggle on a daily bases with material despair. Yet, at the same time, the immigrant's awareness that, somewhere, there is a "land far away" which is filled with all of his aspirations inspires and energizes his existence in the foreign environment.

Immigrants therefore develop and sustain a strong psychological and behavioral orientation towards this "distant land". Edward Said, the Egyptian born American sociologists calls this consciousness an "imaginative geography". He explains that the immigrant's awareness of the "homeland" helps him or her "to intensify its own sense of itself by dramatizing the distance and difference between what is close to it and what is far" and thus keeps them orientated in their foreign setting[1].

In looking for a city with foundation therefore, Abraham was anchoring his lifestyle into the ideals of God's "land". It was this focus that enabled Abraham to fulfill his mission in a foreign environment. Similarly, without locking our life's vision and ambitions into God's system of ethos and rules like Abraham, believers will not live the full life of discipleship to the Lord Jesus Christ. And it was for this reason that the Book of Hebrews describes believers as people who are "longing for a better country" (Heb 11:16).

And this is the essence of Christian discipleship. Jesus demanded that any one who wished to follow Him "must deny himself and take up his cross and follow me" (Mat 16:24). Discipleship to the Lord Jesus, like Abraham's call, requires a spiritual displacement, and movement in a new direction. The people of the world, like those of Babel, may reject and scoff at Jehovah. Yet, God calls upon spiritual descendants of Abraham to live like strangers in "a foreign land". As in the case of Abraham, following Jesus requires uprooting our commitments in life and moving in another direction.

LIVING LIKE A STRANGER IN A FOREIGN LAND

To Abraham's contemporaries, his migration would not have been extraordinary. Immigration, just as it is today, was the fashion of his day. People

---

1. Edward Said, *Orientalism*, London, Penguin Books 1978:55.

moved to and fro, from one end to the other, seeking the best place for their families and herds of cattle to settle. Abraham would have been just like any one of his generation—a man trying his best to get food for his family, make his wife and children happy and ensure that his descendants had a future worth living. Abraham's migration would not have made it into the local papers of his day.

Yet, the news of Abraham's migration made it, not into the local newspapers, but into the eternal records of God Almighty. What made the difference? Three important factors summarize the reasons why Abraham's immigration made it into God's records—God's blessing, Abraham's faith and his obedience.

In commanding Abraham to migrate, God also committed Himself to bless and turn him into a blessing. This blessing on Abraham had three features. Firstly, Abraham became a recipient of God's blessings. He received material blessings from God who promised to give him, "all the land that you see" (Gen 13:14-17). Abraham lost a land in order to inherit another land. He lost family and kindred and property and business. And he inherited God's family, God's kindred, God's property and God's business. Abraham's blessings were evidently material and physical.

Like Abraham, believers who live like strangers in a foreign land by faith and obedience will receive the material provisions of God. Jesus promised that no one who has left home or family for the sake of the kingdom of God "will fail to receive many times as much in this age and, in the age to come, eternal life" (Lk 18:30). When we leave behind the pursuit of the material security and wealth of this world, God will also make sure that we are well catered for. Hence David rightly testified that, "Those who fear [God] lack nothing ... those who seek the LORD lack no good thing" (Ps 34:9-10).

It will be a mistake to brand such a message as a "prosperity and wealth and health" gospel. I do not believe, as some do and preach today, that God somehow owes it to believers to give them money and good health. I deplore the type of preaching that reduces salvation to a material transaction and the gospel of Christ into the gospel of Mammon.

Abraham's life is a testimony to this fact that a life of obedience and faith is not just a matter of wealth, health and prosperity. It came with much pain, deprivation and hardships. When he arrived in the land that God had promised him, his first observation was that the Canaanites were there on the land (Gen 12:6). It took four more centuries for this promise to become a reality. Even after he had obeyed, Abraham suffered famine (Gen 12:10), he was childless for decades, his own nephew quarreled with him, and he was attacked by bandits. Abraham, his servants and possessions were in repeated peril throughout the period of his migration. Because of these hardships Abraham resorted to scheming on two occasions in order to survive. Abraham's life was not the "prosperity and wealth and health" gospel that some preach today.

The Bible however teaches that God takes good care of those who obey and follow Him in faith. He blesses them in physical and material terms. When believers seek God's Kingdom and its righteousness, all the blessings of a caring Father who loves them will be made available. Christian discipleship is living a life of surrender to Christ and trusting fully in Him that He will not leave us nor forsake us. It is therefore equally not right to give the impression that God calls believers to a life of curses and misery. On the contrary, God blesses believers when He calls them to discipleship.

Abraham's blessings were also spiritual. He was called in order to experience a deeper life of fellowship with God. At a time when people called upon idols and set up citadels into heaven to make names for themselves, we are told "The LORD appeared to Abram . . . So he built an altar there to the LORD" (Gen 12:8). That is wonderful. On a land that was idolatrous, the immigrant Abraham begun his mission of building altars for Jehovah and sanctifying the ground for His worship. That is how Christians, aliens of God's Kingdom and immigrants of Christ transform societies.

Abraham was not just a recipient of the blessings of God. He also became a reflector of those blessings. God told him, "I will bless those who bless you, and whoever curses you I will curse" (Gen 12:2–3). The blessings that Abraham received were therefore redirected through him to nations, peoples and lands with which he came into contact. That is how Jehovah operates in the life of the devoted disciple. God chooses a man or woman who would be faithful to Him and turns that person into a mirror and a reflector of His blessings. When God wants to bless a family, He begins with a husband or a wife or a son or a daughter. And through such devoted disciples, His blessings are reflected to others.

This is why Abraham's blessings spilled over to affect people who came into contact with him. Lot, his nephew, was one person who most enjoyed these reflected blessings. God blessed Lot so much, just as He blessed Abraham, that the land could not sustain their properties together.

When Lot chose to live in Sodom and Gomorrah and was captured, it was Abraham who fought and liberated him. When Lot continued in this rather dangerous environment and God brought punishment on those cities, it was through Abraham's intercessory prayer that Lot and his family was spared. Lot received reflected blessings through his uncle Abraham.

In addition to Lot, Abraham's reflected blessings affected Pharaoh, Abimelech, the Canaanites, Ishmael, and Hagar. Every person who had something to do with Abraham, experienced a reflection of God's character, God's blessings and God's anointing on Abraham. Abimelech and his military commanders were absolutely correct when they openly admitted to Abraham, "God is with you in everything you do" (Gen 21:22).

This is how God operates. He blesses our families because we have chosen to follow Him in faith and obedience. He blesses our work colleagues because we continue to hold fast the banner of His love so all peoples may see it. He blesses our cities and countries of residence because we share with Him a close covenantal partnership and so are able to intercede on behalf of others. Christian disciples who follow the Abrahamic way of life are major channels of blessing wherever they happen to be.

And this is the nature of God's strategy of transforming His world. God inserts Christian disciples in places, homes, schools, universities, factories, banks and hospitals. He inserts them into parliament, offices, churches, and into places that one cannot identify. He inserts them there so that through them He would reflect His blessings to the environment and so transform it. God is counting on believers to reflect that glory where He has inserted them.

Disciples of Christ are like "yeast that a woman took and mixed into a large amount of flour until it worked all through the dough" (Mat 13:33). They are the light and the salt that God has inserted in His world. His strategy is that through them, His blessings will be reflected. Paul had a nifty way of putting this concept. He described disciples as "the aroma of Christ among those who are being saved and those who are perishing" (2 Cor 2:15). Aroma, smell, and savor—that is what Christians are to the environment that God has inserted them.

One of the major means through which Abraham became a reflector of God's blessings was the way in which he brought up his children. God said of Abraham that He chose him, so that he will direct his children and his household "to keep the way of the LORD by doing what is right and just" (Gen 18:19). God's strategy was to bless the world through the descendants of Abraham. Abraham's responsibility in this covenantal strategy was to train and instruct his children to love and fear Jehovah God. In so doing faith and love for God would spread throughout the earth. And this exactly is how God intends to bless the world. Through Christian parents who fear and love God and studiously bring up their children to do the same, the blessings of God will be reflected throughout the whole earth.

Abraham did not just receive and reflect God's blessings, he also radiated it. God turned him into a blessing. There is a difference between a reflector and a radiator. Whereas a reflector only reflects the light it receives, a radiator provides heat with it. A radiator is a source of energy. God told him, *"by you all the families of the earth shall bless themselves"* (Gen 12:3 NRSV). In other words the mention of Abraham's name will bring blessings to people. This is an extravagant promise of God indeed.

And Abraham proved this in real life. When Pharaoh seized his wife, God punished Pharaoh's house. When Abimelech tried it again, God punished him also. God spoke to Abimelech in a dream, "You are as good as dead" (Gen 20:3). "Anyone who curses you will be cursed"—that was what was happening to Abimelech. When Abimelech repented of his evil intentions, Abraham laid hands on him and he was healed. That is what God turns people who love and fear Him into. They become satellite sources of blessings.

Disciples of Christ, who live like strangers in a foreign land, become fountains of God's blessings. From them will flow God's touch of healing to the society. They are sources of restoration, of grace, of renewal and revival in the land. They are the people God uses to turn the world upside down. That was the project into which God called Abraham. And we share this calling with him.

WALKING BY FAITH AND OBEDIENCE

The main distinguishing feature of Abraham's life as an immigrant was his faith and obedience. His faith was one that took God at His word. We first notice this when God showered extravagant promises of posterity and land on him. God told Abraham, "Look up at the heavens and count the stars ... So shall your offspring be" (Gen 15:5). Who would believe such an excessive promise? Yet, Abraham did. Abraham's faith was so immensely simple that the modern cynical person may dismiss it as naïve. Abraham decided that when it came to faith in Jehovah, he was not going to be sophisticated at all about it. He would let God be true and every man be a liar. That was the nature of Abraham's friendship with God.

Though simple, Abraham's faith, was not a foolish a one. This is because it was based on a deep knowledge of the character and covenantal love of Jehovah God. Abraham reasoned to himself, "This God whom I worship, He is a just God. He does not lie, and is not a tease. This God I worship does not boast, does not bluff, does not need to impress anybody, and does not owe me anything. He does not depend on me in any way. Therefore if my God has gone out of His way to give me His promises, what reasons do I have not to believe Him? I do believe because I know my God to be who He is, the Lord of all the earth, with whom nothing is impossible. If He has said it, will He not do it?"

Several Christians struggle with believing God for three main reasons—they do not rely on the Word of God. Or when they do, they do not rely on the character of God. Or they forget about God's Covenant. These three were the secrets behind Abraham's faith. When life is hard, it is easy for believers to fall into the trap of believing our imaginations, and trusting our own calculations and expectations. It becomes easy for wishful thinking to take over and for us to put words into God's mouth and to then expect Him to fulfill these wishes. That is not faith, and that is certainly not the nature of Abraham's faith. Faith builds its foundations on the Word of God. It does not embellish, exaggerate, or make it say what we wish to hear.

After we have believed His Word, we need to continue believing because of God's character. His character makes Him someone who will not change His mind. His character makes Him someone who binds Himself to His own promises. So when He has spoken, we should be sure that it will happen. Abraham believed God because He accepted God's character as genuine, untainted and reliable.

Abraham's faith was not just based on God's Word, and God's character; it was also based on God's covenant. In Gen 15, where we get this record that Abraham believed and God credited it to him as righteousness, his faith was confirmed with a covenant sealing ceremony (Gen 15:18). From then on Abraham knew that God's promises were bound, not only to His character but also to His covenant, and to His oath. We can also be sure and have faith in the Word of God because God has sealed His promises to us with His covenant.

Abraham

Abraham did not only believe; He also obeyed. After the first command from God in Gen 12, we are told, "So Abram left, as the LORD had told him" (Gen 12:4). How simple is this man's discipleship. He didn't ask any questions. He threw no tantrums, and he didn't request for any assurances. Abraham obeyed God without any "if"s and "but"s. He made no hesitation, or reservations when obeying God. Abraham just got up and went, "as the LORD had told him". He should have written a book titled "Obedience made simple"!

This was not the only occasion in Abraham's life in which he demonstrates this unquestioningly simplified and unhesitant obedience. In Gen 22, we are told God came to Abraham and commanded him to go and sacrifice his son. This command, we must admit, is the most shocking command from God in the whole Bible. The writer softens our shock by prefacing the command with the warning that it was a "test" from God. For Abraham however, there was no preface at all. Though we, the readers, are told that it was a test from God, Abraham on the other hand was not forewarned about the test. That makes this command very dreadful—at least it should have been to Abraham.

So what should Abraham do about this shocking command? Shouldn't he ask for a few more details about Moriah, about which mountain, and about the procedure? Shouldn't he find out what happens now to God's promises since Isaac, according to God, was the one through whom those promises would be fulfilled? Shouldn't he examine why he needed to travel for three days to Moriah? Yet, Abraham didn't do any of these. Instead, the Bible tells us that Abraham set off the next morning to Moriah to perform the sacrifice.

It is not as if Abraham is slavish in his relationship with Jehovah. When it was necessary, Abraham questioned and bargained and pleaded and challenged God to remain true to His character. For example, before this incident, Abraham had confronted and haggled with God over Sodom and Gomorrah. He challenged God, "Will not the judge of all the earth do right?" (Gen 18:25). Why then, did Abraham not do the same when it came to obedience?

Abraham obeyed because he trusted God. The fact is there is no true obedience if it is not acted out of faith. Every demand from God is a test of our faith and every act of so-called obedience that is not done out of faith fails that test in the first place. Abraham had this faith (James 2:21–22). He believed in the resurrection, so He was willing to sacrifice his son. He believed in the power of the Word of God so he trusted that God would speak and his son will come alive again. Abraham believed the character of God and so He acted in obedience.

Abraham's obedience was also a covenantal obedience. His walk with God was based on a covenant of friendship, of deep love and affection. Because of this, Abraham knew that no command comes from God without this covenantal love. And within that covenant, Abraham's responsibility was to obey. Abraham did not ask any questions of God because all the questions had been answered already within the covenant between him and Jehovah.

Obedience will be straightforward to God's children if we were to constantly remind ourselves of Calvary's covenant. If we were to experience and know on a daily basis how much God loves us, no commandment from Him will be so unreasonable, so reckless, and so shocking to us. What else can beat the shock of God giving up his own Son to die in our place on the cross? What more does God have to do to show that he loves us?

Jesus has demonstrated to us how much He loves us by laying down His life for us (Jn 15:13). Now, as His friends, He calls upon us to obey His commandments. It is when our relationship with God becomes a practical living out of this covenant of friendship, that obedience becomes less convoluted. When we too have come to the place of deep friendship with Him, then we will be enabled to obey like Abraham.

DISCUSSION QUESTIONS

1. There is a common saying within some Christian circles that some believers are too "heavenly minded" to be of any earthly use. How does Abraham's life disprove this notion and show instead that if we are properly heavenly minded we would always be of use on earth?

2. What do you think about Abraham's behavior as an immigrant in Egypt?

3. Faith, for Abraham, was a matter of relying on God's Word, God's Covenant and God's Character. Explain how each one of these contributes to our own faith.

Joseph

*You Intended to Harm Me but God Intended It for Good:
Turning Your Bitter Experiences into Good*

In the 1994 Hollywood film titled "Forrest Gump", one of the many words of wisdom to have come from the mouth of witless Gump, played by the actor Tom Hanks, was this—"My momma always said, "Life was like a box of chocolates. You never know what you're gonna get." Not many people will dispute with this statement of wisdom. All of us are exposed in varying degrees to a mixture of the good and the bad, the happy and the sad occasions. It is the lot of all human beings that life is indeed a box of chocolates of different shades of sweetness. It is true that some are more harshly treated by life than others. However, we all at some point in life are dished some bitterness and hardship.

The difference between success and failure is in how we respond and deal with the bitter experiences in life. Some respond to the difficulty of life by being aggressive, sour, unforgiving and even lash out their frustration on others. Others respond by being reactive, defeatist and passive, and full of despair. Still others respond with positive determination and refreshing energy to restart life again. They respond with a constructive attitude that enables them to transform their bitterness into sweetness. It is the manner in which we react to the bitter experiences in life that dictates the success.

This lack of ability to control what happens in one's life is exceptionally true for the immigrant. Life for the immigrant is a constant exposure to chance. The immigrant's life depends on which "chocolate" he randomly picks from the box! In addition to being at the mercy of the lottery of life, the immigrant also lacks the resources to buffer the bitterness that may result. Due to his rootlessness, the immigrant does not have as much community capital and social security to cushion him against the difficult problems of life. When life therefore turns bitter, the downward spiral for the immigrant can be very swift indeed.

The story of Joseph that is recorded in Genesis 37–50, is a dramatic illustration of how to turn the bitter experiences in life to good. This young ambitious "dreamer" learnt that life was not just a matter of "dream it and claim it and it happens". Joseph experienced the lowest of the immigrant condition. He experienced rejection, persecution and hatred by his own relatives. He was banished, isolated in slavery, was betrayed, falsely imprisoned, and ended up in the lowest dungeon of Egypt. Joseph had every excuse in the book to develop the "victim mentality".

Yet, out of the deepest prison of life, Joseph rose to become the prime minister of Egypt. His Spirit inspired wisdom was to save not only the foreign country where he had immigrated to but also his own family back where he had come from. This boy had every reason to feel victimized by life, persecuted by his family, mistreated by his employer, and offended by God. Instead, Joseph beams throughout the chapters of Genesis 37–50 with a sense of calmness and confidence, and even positive expectation.

In addition, Joseph became the instrument through whom God protected His people at a time of world economic crisis. Supposing Joseph had buckled under the pressure and responded to his harsh experiences with equal bitterness and anger against God, what a massive difference the story could have turned out to be. We never know how much our courage may turn out as blessings on generations to come.

What was the secret of Joseph's success? How did he manage to turn his dreams into reality? Five features from the story of Joseph provide us the answers to these questions—Joseph was driven by a dream, pruned by suffering, proved by his moral courage, interpreted his life from God's perspective and was favoured by God.

DRIVEN BY A DREAM

The story of Joseph begins in Gen 37 with a description of a dysfunctional family in which the head of household openly showed favoritism to one of his younger sons. In addition, this favored son began having dreams that suggested that he would, in future, be the leader. Joseph then worsened the already fragile situation by blatantly bragging about his dreams. Unsurprisingly, on four occasions in the opening eleven verses of the story, the Bible repeats the refrain that Joseph's brothers "hated him and could not speak a kind word to him" (Gen 37:4, 5, 8, 11). What was the significance of Joseph's dreams? How did the dreams contribute to building up his character?

Though we are not explicitly told how Joseph relied on his dreams, there can be no doubt that his persistence was partly a result of the confidence that came from the dreams. Joseph's two dreams would certainly have been at the back of his mind as he went through the dark stages of his life. The dreams stimulated a vision of possibilities. They fuelled an imagination for achieving great things. And this goal driven life was a major factor in this young man's success.

Some may argue that, perhaps, Joseph already harbored ambitions before God showed him his dreams. Judging from his behavior after having the dreams, this is possible. Undoubtedly, his parents and brothers saw things that way. In a household that was heading for internal destruction through sibling rivalry, a desire for order was a good thing. If Joseph therefore had ambitions to restore order in the family, God was acknowledging and strengthening them through the dreams.

The fact is the story of the transformation of every society begins with a dreamer. Transformation begins when a man or woman has a positive vision, and imagination to change things. Those who lack this imagination fail their organizations. On the other hand, those who have it save them from failure. Joseph had it and God confirmed and crystallized it.

One positive characteristic of the immigrant, at least the successful immigrant, is his capacity for dreaming. Having experienced the harshness of life, the immigrant cannot but start dreaming of change. Moreover, because of his previous encounters with other cultures, the immigrant is usually more willing to consider various other ways of seeing things and solving problems. It may be that this capacity for imagination and "dreaming" is one factor that makes the immigrant a suitable agent of transformation.

God indeed regards ambitions that are aimed at building up His people as noble (1 Tim 3:1). In Christendom today, we are tending to make two types of errors in relation to this whole matter of ambitions. Either we lack ambition, or when we have it, we do not use it in the service of God's Kingdom. There are believers who are not driven by any objectives related to fulfilling the great commission. They are like the disciples in John 4 whose imaginations were blinded to the "ripe fields" (Jn 4:35).

Like the disciples, these believers busy themselves with self-preservation and fail to see God's hand at work in their circumstances.

Yet, the imagination is so important if believers are to flourish as God's change agents. Indeed, faith thrives on the imagination. It is when we keep imagining and seeing with our inner eye, the promises that we hear from God's Word that our faith flourishes. So Paul prayed for the Ephesians, that "the eyes of your heart may be enlightened" in order to know God's hope (Eph 1:18–19). If Christians of today are to transform the places where God has inserted them, they also need the same "enlightenment of the eye of the heart". Believers fail the Lord Jesus when they sit on their hands and keep saying, "it is not possible, it has never been done this way before, it is much too difficult and it is not yet time". And so their churches, families and communities continue to fall apart.

Thankfully, Joseph had an ambition that did not accept the disorder in his family. What Joseph lacked however, was the constraining power of God's Spirit to channel his ambitions properly. This is the aspect of the dreams that Joseph, his father and his brothers failed to understand. Instead of carefully seeking God's direction and the guidance of trusted people, Joseph went about bragging about his dreams to his brothers. He never pondered how his brothers would feel about the dreams. Joseph had not learnt that dream sharing is an occasion for humility, and not for gloating.

Joseph's problem was not lack of ambitions. His problem was an ambition that was not humbled and constrained by love and consideration for others. His ambitions were not shaped by the fruit of the Spirit. Like him believers need to appreciate that their ambitions must be constrained by humility and consideration for others. Christian disciples should not trample on others, wipe their noses in the mud and manipulate them to achieve "noble" ambitions. Not even the excuse of a dream or a revelation from God justifies having to manipulate and harm the egos of others.

Joseph's subsequent experience taught him how to let the Spirit of God constrain his ambitions. From this point on, God took over this young man's ambitions, pruned him and made him fit for His service. Every Christian needs this pruning process.

PRUNED BY SUFFERING

If Joseph expected that the dreams would be immediately fulfilled without much tears, he was in for a big disappointment. Instead of his family rejoicing with him, his brothers hated him more. They then sold him to be a slave in a foreign land. The prince of Jacob with big ambitions of domination, turned into the slave of Potiphar, right at the bottom of the pile in a strange land. Joseph learnt that though vision is important, it was only the beginning of the hard work of fulfillment. Jesus promised that every believer who bears fruit, "God prunes so that he will be even more fruitful" (Jn 15:2). And so Joseph learnt how God prunes His servants through the suffering he experienced.

Some of the troubles that Joseph went through were the consequences of his own actions. In repeatedly bragging to his brothers about his dreams, Joseph was inviting jealousy and hostility from them. It may be only slightly harsh to say that he brought some of his problems upon himself. Similarly, when we disobey God's law or flout the laws of the country, the resulting pain is our fault. When a Christian over-speeds or parks his car at the wrong place he should not be surprised about the penalty. Likewise, when we presume on the grace of God and sin, we are sowing seeds that will grow and bear the fruits of hardships.

Whereas most Christians agree that "we reap what we sow", some struggle on occasions to deal with the pain that result from their errors. They instead respond with frustration, bitterness and even anger for what has clearly resulted from their own mistakes. They find it difficult to take the result of the sin on the chin and get on with repairing the damage. Somehow some believers underestimate the immense seriousness of the blunders we commit. Perhaps we stubbornly expect God to always cover up and clean up our messes. Joseph was to learn that what may appear to be a very little mistake could end up in a big chaos whose consequences may be far reaching beyond our generation.

However, not all of life's troubles are due to our own faults. Some are clearly through no fault of ours. The actions and decisions of those who have authority over us may, from time to time, result in our suffering. It was no fault of Joseph's that his father showed him open favoritism. It was not his fault that his brothers hated him and so sold him into slavery. It was no fault of his that Potiphar's wife was attracted to him. It was not Joseph's fault that the Pharaoh's butler was ungrateful. Joseph learnt the meaning of suffering unjustly through the fault of others.

This, I fear, is the depressing lot of humanity—we all sometimes suffer through no fault of ours. We experience suffering because we are children of Adam. So a husband's mistake could have more serious consequences for his wife and children than himself. A doctor's error could result in immense suffering to an innocent patient. A government's inconsiderate or unjust law or action could result in the pain and suffering of innocent citizens of a country.

Believers, like Joseph need to learn, that even in these particular circumstances, God still uses suffering to prune us and sharpen us. As the story progressed, Joseph learnt by Gen 48, that though the suffering we may go through are not within our control, the sovereign Lord, who rules over all that happens in our lives, is in control of our destiny. He will never get it wrong with regard to the children He loves. We can therefore continue to trust Him, humble ourselves under His mighty hand and persevere onto the end. We can stand firm under unjust suffering because the Lord God is in control of all of them.

Joseph experienced a third type of suffering during his pruning experience. He suffered as a result of believing in God. Joseph suffered for doing the right thing. He went to prison, not because he had broken any laws or rejected any of God's commandments. Joseph went into prison because he feared God. His main reason for resisting Potiphar's wife were not because he feared he would be caught, or that he might lose his job or even that he had too much respect for his boss not to offend him. Joseph's main reason, which perhaps most infuriated the woman, was because he feared God (Gen 39:9). It must have been very painful for him to be in prison knowing that he was there because of his fear of God.

Many Christians may accept suffering that is their fault, or even when it is evident that the pain is one of natural consequences and affects all humanity. What some struggle to deal with is the suffering that comes after they have obeyed God. We fail to grasp what Paul told the Philippians, that their calling was not only to believe in Christ, but also to suffer for him (Phil 1:29). We easily accept the first part of believing in Him, but not the second part of suffering for Him.

It is interesting that it was not until Gen 39 that we first hear Joseph bring God into his affairs. After suffering hardships through his own fault, the fault of others and for the sake of his faith in God, Joseph was now pruned and ready to be God's instrument of transformation. He had now learnt the way of the Lord God that brings strength and courage to enable His disciple to stand. That is what suffering does for us as believers. The Book of Hebrews says that suffering "produces a harvest of righteousness and peace for those who have been trained by it" (Heb 12:11). "Harvest of righteousness" is what we now see in the new Joseph in Gen 39.

PROVED BY MORAL COURAGE

Joseph was not only pruned by the suffering he experienced. He was also proved as true by the temptations and trials he underwent. Coping with suffering and resisting bitterness and anger is one thing. Standing firm on one's moral principles and refusing to compromise regardless of the consequences is however of a higher order. Suffering prunes us so that within ourselves we develop firm inner integrity and morality. By Gen 39, Joseph had developed this moral integrity.

At some point in every disciple's life, we will have to prove that we are not all just talk-talk but are real devotees of the Lord Jesus. At some point, we will have to show the mettle of which we are made. Our internal moral fiber, our integrity and spiritual courage must one day be displayed. A day comes in every disciple of Christ's life when we have to be tested to show that we indeed are ready for the higher responsibilities of being God's ambassadors. And that day came for Joseph when Potiphar's wife subjected him to sexual harassment.

Joseph's response to Potiphar's wife in Gen 39:8–9 demonstrates his integrity, purity and obedience to God. Integrity means completeness, and wholeness. It describes a person who fits together. A person of integrity has no fakery in him. His behavior is consistent with the general character that he or she espouses. Integrity is not spinning one's way through life and telling people what they want to hear. Instead, it is honesty and truthfulness. It is feeling bound by one's word and doing everything possible to fulfill one's promises

Joseph had that quality and hence Potiphar did not concern himself with anything in the house. Joseph was a trustworthy worker who could be relied upon to turn up for work on time, get on with it and achieve his targets before the deadlines. His accounting was straightforward and uncomplicated. He didn't take anything that did not belong to him. Hence his master had absolute confidence in him. Joseph worked hard to deserve this trust and confidence from his employer.

One of the letdowns of today's Christianity, it is sad to say, is the failure of this emphasis on integrity as the trademark of the disciple of Christ. In his book, *The Scandal of the Evangelical Conscience*, Ronald J

Sider laments this failure in America. Sider points out that, "Scandalous behavior is rapidly destroying American Christianity. By their daily activity, most "Christians" regularly commit treason. With their mouths they claim that Jesus is Lord, but with their actions they demonstrate allegiance to money, sex and self-fulfillment".[1] This is true not just of America but also of other countries of the world. Not a week passes without a scandal being reported in the newspapers of the world involving prominent Christians caught out embezzling funds or involved in other forms of scandalous behavior.

Why is this happening? One reason is our failure to emphasize integrity as the hallmark of the disciple of Christ in our fellowships. Because we are counting the effectiveness of our ministries in terms of numbers—just as the world does its business; we have stopped emphasizing the difficult and hard things that Jesus requires of His disciples. Alan Wolfe, the Director of the Biosi Centre of Religion and American Public Life, poignantly summarizes this state of affairs when he says this about postmodern Christianity—"The truth is there is increasingly little difference between an essentially secular activity like the popular entertainment industry and the bring-'em-in-at-any-cost efforts of evangelical megachurches".[2]

We should have known that a Christianity that makes the acquisition of wealth as the trademark of "big" faith in Christ will sooner than later fall into the trap of cutting corners and making the end justify the means. When we regard ourselves in competition with the world on worldly goods, we will very rapidly find ourselves also in competition with them on how to cheat and lie and spin our ways through the difficult moral mazes of life. Short cuts have helped nobody, not the least the Church of Christ.

Joseph's motivation in refusing to sleep with Mrs. Potiphar was more than an inner commitment to integrity and personal purity. Joseph's action was simply in obedience to God. He knew he would have been flouting God's law and disobeying His commandments. And ambassadors of God, His change agents in the world, don't do that. God expects aliens of His kingdom to call sin by its name and to repudiate it.

Though many Christians know this; yet, on a daily basis, some of us ignore His wishes. During a stage of His ministry, the Lord bitterly com-

1. Ronald J Sider, *The Scandal of the Evangelical Conscience* Baker Books, Grand Rapids, Michigan, 2005:12–13.

2. Alan Wolfe, *The Transformation of American Religion: How We Actually Live Our Faith,* New York, Free Press, 2003:212.

plained about the attitude of some of His followers. These were people who majored in shouting about how wonderful their salvation was, and yet ignored what He taught them. So the Lord protested, "Why do you call me, "Lord, Lord", and do not do what I say?" (Lk 6:46). Imagine the tears of disappointment in His loving eyes as He spoke those words!

INTERPRETING LIFE FROM GOD'S PERSPECTIVE

Having gone through the bitter pruning and tough proving experiences, Joseph became a successful ambassador for God in a foreign land. Yet, Joseph was of use to God's people only because he regarded his daily affairs, the dealings of his family and occupation as fitting into God's plan. Joseph considered every bit of his circumstances as having something to do with God's agenda in his life. To Pharaoh's butler, he attributed the gift of interpretation of dreams to God (Gen 40:8). He openly confessed his faith in Jehovah to Pharaoh, "I cannot do it, but God will give Pharaoh the answer" (Gen 41:16). Joseph acknowledged that his success was due to the fact that God was in every aspect of his life. Again and again in Gen 39, we are told "The LORD was with Joseph and he prospered" (Gen 39:2, 3, & 5).

Certainly, Joseph's rise to prominence in Egypt could not have come about just through his personal abilities, even his integrity and purity, but through God's hand that was on him. And he acknowledged it in his everyday dealings. Like Joseph, believers may serve God's purposes only when they perceive things in the way God perceives them. It is when believers relate to their experiences, whether bitter or sweet, as if God is physically present in the situation, that they would make a difference to their environment.

That is the philosophy with which Joseph approached life in Egypt. So when his brothers came to Egypt, he told them, "it was not you who sent me here, but God" (Gen 45:8). Is that really true? Wasn't it the Midianite slave traders who sent Joseph to Egypt? Was Joseph not in Egypt because he was recruited as a labourer in Potiphar's estates? Wasn't it his brothers who envied and hated him and sold him to the traders? Wasn't it his ambitions and dreams and integrity and purity; his skills at dream interpretation and his good networking connections in the prison that made him what he was? Wasn't Joseph paraded before Pharaoh because he was a highly skilled migrant worker experienced in the interpretation of dreams? Was Joseph not spinning a yarn in claiming that it was God who sent him there into Egypt?

Certainly not! Joseph wasn't spinning. In God's perspective, and in God's strategy, it was God who put Joseph where he was. Joseph was aware of the twisted hands of his brothers in his immigration to Egypt. Yet, He also knew of the powerful Hand of the Sovereign God in his immigration. He told them, "God sent me ahead of you to preserve for you a remnant on earth and to save your lives by a great deliverance" (Gen 45:7). That, to me, is a most profound, God inspired statement by this thirty year old man in a foreign country. Joseph understood that he was where he was to fulfill God's agenda, to serve God's purpose and fulfill His programme. He knew that he was not in Egypt by chance.

Imagine the difference they would make if the many Christians who have risen to high positions—Christian doctors, Christian university professors, Christian politicians, Christian administrators, Christian accountants, Christian economists, Christian novelists, Christian journalists, Christian army officers—imagine what a revolution would occur if each and everyone of us were to interpret our lives that way. Visualize how much transformation we will see in our homes and offices, if we were to start strategizing and implementing our choices with God's agenda as the overriding focus. That is what it means to be an alien of the kingdom of God.

Christian immigrants may be where they are now because of several reasons. Like Joseph, they may have been recruited as skilled migrant workers. On the other hand, they may be refugees, asylum seekers or economic migrants. Yet, they are more than these. In God's strategy, Christian immigrants are where they are because of something specific to do with God's Kingdom. They are God's missionaries and change agents in the environments into which God has placed them today. Like Joseph, Christian immigrants need to interpret their experiences through God's perspective.

Before we think that Joseph was an exceptional case, reflect on his failures. Joseph was as fallible as every human being. We have already described his unrestrained ambition and his lack of the fruit of the Spirit. In another odd twist to the story in Gen 42–44, Joseph again treated his brothers with similar inconsideration and deeply hurt his father. Having been badly maltreated by his brothers in the past, Joseph seemed to be obsessed with distrusting them. And in that situation, the old bitterness resurfaced. In treating them so harshly in Gen 42-44, Joseph was acting a bit like his brothers. Except that he didn't want to kill them!

Joseph, the man of success, struggled to be totally magnanimous to his repentant brothers, unless it was on his own terms. It was only after Judah's inspired speech in Gen 44:18-34 that Joseph became convicted and changed his attitude towards his brothers and forgave them. The man or woman of the Spirit should not behave as Joseph did at a time of triumph. Joseph was fallible, no different from us.

Yet, he was overwhelmingly successful. And in his success he gave God the credit and the glory. He told Pharaoh "I cannot do it but God will give Pharaoh the answer he desires" (Gen 41:16). Pharaoh therefore had any choice but to recognize the operation of the Spirit of God in Joseph. When he sent for his father into Egypt, Joseph gave this message—"God has made me lord of all Egypt" (Gen 45:9). That is the secret of the success of Christ's ambassadors in this world.

FAVORED BY GOD

There is one more factor that determined Joseph's success as an immigrant. For, we can be sure that at the time, Joseph was not the only foreigner who came to Egypt. Even within his family, God had a choice among twelve boys, to use to preserve His covenant people. God wanted to preserve His people and chose Joseph as the particular person to receive the dreams, and to send to Egypt. Why did God choose Joseph and not the others?

The fact is Joseph rose to prominence and success simply because God favored him. And that is the message around which the whole story of Joseph in Gen 37-50 revolves. Ultimately, if one is not being irreverent in saying so, God seems to have behaved in Gen 37-50, just like Jacob. God favored Joseph as the person He had chosen for His strategy of transformation. God specifically chose to preserve and strengthen Joseph through the difficult times to fulfill His eternal purposes.

Jacob was wrong in his favoritism, and he cannot be excused. God is however never wrong in choosing, predestining and electing believers before the beginning of the world. He is never wrong in appointing us to be His favored ones in this world, to be His ambassadors of transformation. Reflect on this, that God is never wrong in choosing you above all others for the special task He has destined for you where He has placed you.

The God of the Bible is full of such inscrutable and strange behavior—in favoring, electing and choosing people for no special qualifications or extraordinary abilities they possess. He just pours His favor on the people He chooses and works things out for their good. To these people, on whom His favor dwells, who are called to fulfill His purposes, and who love Him, the Bible says, "in all things God works for the good" (Rom 8:28).

And why do these people love God? They do love Him only because He first loved them. Why is that? Why has He done it even when these people were rebels and rejecters of His love? Why does God persist with them even when they fail Him? Who knows the mind of God? Who can tell His deep wisdom and impenetrable foreknowledge in favoring undeserving and often rejected people with His love?

Over the centuries, many Christians have struggled to understand this doctrine of God's foreknowledge and election. Yet, Jacob understood and knew it as an experience. He had learnt that, though he was a lazy schemer and a cheat, he was favored over and above his hardworking brother Esau. Jacob knew how God had disapproved of his stealing and trickery and made him suffer for it in banishment and slave labor under the equal deception and trickery of his uncle Laban. Yet, Jacob was also conscious of how God forgave and overruled the consequences of his evil deeds and favored and blessed him.

Judah, in these fourteen chapters of Genesis, also learnt about this extraordinary character of God. The prostitution story in Gen 38 has been put there by God as a key in teaching us about His strange and mysterious ways. No novelist could have invented such a bizarre but true event—that eventually King David and the Lord Jesus should be descendants of Tamar. This foreign Canaanite woman dressed herself as a prostitute in Gen 38 in order to sleep with Judah her father-in-law. And the resulting baby became an ancestor of Jesus. What an amazing story!

By the time Judah gave his long speech in Gen 44, which convicted Joseph of his harshness, he had also learnt by experience that, for those called to fulfill God's purposes, those who love Him, God turns human evil into Divine good. God sometimes turns the bitter experiences and even blunders of his favored ones into good.

Joseph himself, at the final stages of the story in Gen 48, also learnt about this extraordinary behavior of God. He learnt that God chooses undeserving marginalized people above the world's favorites. He picks up those the world has rejected and excluded and then favors them.

Joseph

When Joseph brought his sons to be blessed by Jacob, he thought God would confirm the usual practice, the normal expectations, and the fashionable procedures. Joseph was however mistaken. He tried to change the situation, but he couldn't for Jacob outwit him. Actually, it was God who outwitted Joseph and chose the younger Ephraim above the older Manasseh. Why did God favor the rejected Ephraim? No one can tell. What we can know however is that when God favors a man or woman, no other person can cancel it out. Balaam was right in telling Balak, "How can I curse those whom God has not cursed?" (Num 23:8).

As Christian immigrants are faced with various kinds of bitter experiences in their host countries, they do well to bear God's favor in mind. As believers struggle to bear testimony in their difficult situations, they need to remember God's favor as the main ingredient of success. Jesus said, "You did not choose me, but I chose you and appointed you" (Jn 15:16). We are children of God, not because some time ago we took decisions to put our faith in Jesus. That is not correct theology. According to Jesus, we are Christians, only because He chose us before the foundation of the world to become His own.

Like Joseph, we are favored so that we will be used to fulfill His agenda in our particular situations. Let us avoid his mistake of triumphalism. Let us instead, allow the fruit of His Spirit to humble us and lead us to fulfill His strategies where He has placed us.

DISCUSSION QUESTIONS

1. By what criteria should we judge whether our ambitions and visions are correct?
2. In what sense did God show favoritism on Joseph? Does this type of predestination and choice contradict God's fairness?
3. As a migrant worker in Egypt, Joseph did excel in his duties under his rather unjust boss. What do you think should be our reaction and attitude to our employers who, regardless of our efforts, treat us unfairly?

Israel

Let My People Go So They Will Worship Me in the Desert:
Experiencing God's Power in Life's Wilderness

For many immigrants, life in their new countries often feels like traveling through the wilderness. They may occasionally come across an oasis of fresh water to drink. From time to time, they may find a palm tree under whose shade they might rest from the hot weather. A growing fruit whose juices may restore their energies and revive thoughts of a possible end to their ordeals may sporadically be stumbled upon. Nevertheless, by and large, the rootlessness, social exclusion, discrimination, and internal confusion make the immigrant life comparable to wandering through the wilderness.

Almost universally, most immigrants do repeat this wilderness experience when they enter their new environment. The troubles, for some, begin even before they enter the host countries. Regardless of the reasons for immigration, the financial difficulties involved in organizing the move is often crippling in the short to medium term. These difficulties do put significant pressures on immigrants to quickly raise money in the shortest possible time. Occasionally, they need to defray debts and send money home to their families. Finding a job to provide this money, even for the highly skilled migrant, is not always easy.

It is frequently not long before the immigrant realizes that, contrary to the stories they had heard, the financial grass was not as green on the other side. Most immigrants soon become aware that milk and honey do not flow on the gold paved streets of their new countries.

For those immigrants who find jobs, some continue to struggle with the harsh realities of working as minority persons in new countries. They are shocked to realize that the rules often operate differently for them as compared to other people with similar or even inferior qualifications. It becomes a common experience for the immigrant to be bypassed for promotion, denied interviews or even inadequately remunerated for their work. For some, complaining may only make their lot worse. So daily work may only serve as a reminder of an immigrant's "differentness".

For others, it is the bitter social experience of isolation and loneliness that makes immigration a wilderness experience. Not knowing many people in their neighborhoods, some immigrants do find their first few years in their new countries extremely challenging. The prejudice and unfairness makes this social exclusion even more real. It does not take long for the anxieties, emotional trauma and hardship to take their toll in causing depression and psychological problems for the immigrant.

The huge number of psychological ailments that many immigrants develop has been carefully documented by John W Berry in his magisterial article titled *Acculturation and Adaptation in a New Society,* published in 1992 in the journal, *International Migrations.* According to Berry, immigrants experience immense psychological stresses and problems including "lowered mental health status (particularly anxiety and depression), feelings of marginality and alienation, and heightened psychosomatic and psychological symptoms"[1].

Similarly, Ihsan Al-Issa and Michel Tousignant in their book, *Ethnicity, Immigration, and Psychopathology* thoroughly researched and compared the lives and experiences of all the immigrant groups scattered in various countries of the world. They concluded that all immigrants experience major cultural and emotional "stressors that are unique to them"[2]. The immigrant's experience of considerable psychological and emotional strains in a strange land feels indeed like wandering in the wilderness.

One of the most difficult experiences that many Christian immigrants encounter is finding a suitable church for fellowship. On occasions, through lack of sensitivity, some church members have actually given immigrants the impression that they are not welcome to the fellowship. The existence of the "megachurch" phenomenon tends to exacerbate this isolation. For, in these rather large churches, the possibility that a new immigrant could be identified and ministered to effectively diminishes.

1. John W Berry, "Acculturation and Adaptation in a new society", International Migrations, 1992 (30): 69–84; p. 75.

2. Ihsan Al-Issa and Michel Tousignant, Ethnicity, Immigration, and Psychopathology Plenum Press, New York 1997:13.

A number of immigrants soon find that, even when they feel welcome to a church fellowship, it takes considerable effort to adjust to the different style of Christian worship. A seemingly higher than average emphasis on social issues, over against "spiritual stimulation", does disappoint some immigrants. In addition, the immigrant's nostalgia for a different worship style may make fellowshipping with the church unexciting. Several immigrants may find that it doesn't make a big difference to their spiritual wellbeing whether they went to church or not. Others resort to moving from church to church with no established roots, spiritual discipline or effective fellowship with other believers.

For many immigrants, the lack of an effective fellowship begins a process of what is often called "the spiritual wilderness". This is at times compounded by the feeling of guilt and spiritual alienation that comes with resorting to habits and actions that are not in tune with God's will. Not a few immigrants adopt Abraham's discredited strategy when he decided to go to Egypt as an economic migrant. And with such behavior and actions come the constant sense of guilt and estrangement from God that feels very much like the spiritual wilderness.

At this stage, several immigrants begin to find it difficult to pray and study the Word of God. Instead, they plunge themselves into the "rat race" and constantly struggle with as many jobs as they can get. God begins to be frozen out of their lives and so are the children of God. To them, God now seems aloof and disinterested in their struggles. When they pray, it feels as if their prayers hit a wall just above them and return back without any effect. The daily quiet time is shuffled out of their busy schedules and even when they manage to have one it is as dry as reading the Yellow Pages.

For quite a few Christian believers, this may be the beginning of great doubts about their faith in the Lord Jesus. They may start to question whether they had not taken "the whole Bible thing" too seriously. They begin to wonder whether God is as interested in their affairs as they had assumed. They then consider whether they should adopt the general philosophy of the people they meet on a daily basis—people who have no God in their lives, and who just work hard and pursue their dreams and appear to be rewarded in the end. Several Christian immigrants fall into this trap, and begin to reject their Christian faith and ethos.

Every year, this unhappy depiction of the slippery slope of immigration is repeated all over the world. Yet, it is not a new phenomenon. For, since biblical times, immigration has always been experienced as a life of wandering through the wilderness. Indeed, the above portrayal of immigration as a wilderness experience is comparable to what the children of Israel encountered after their liberation from Egypt. The Bible says, while they were in Egypt, they groaned in their slavery and cried out to God. He looked down on their misery and intervened to save them by setting them on a journey of migration to another land.

One of the main reasons for Israel's migration was the severe oppression in Egypt. Most migrant people today in contrast, leave their countries of birth for economic and social reasons. It is true though, that a proportion of people migrate because of oppression and persecution in their homeland. Regardless of the reasons for their exodus however, most of today's immigrants are bound to see their exodus in biblical terms. Like Israel, most immigrants regard their exodus as liberation from a life of hardship and difficulties to a "Promised Land" which is full of their positive aspirations. The story of the liberation of biblical Israel is therefore being interpreted on a daily basis among immigrants of today's world.

What lessons can Christian immigrants learn from the exodus of Israel through the wilderness? The migration experience of Israel, as recorded in Exodus, Leviticus, Numbers and Deuteronomy, teaches Christian immigrants of today two broad lessons—it teaches about the dangers, as well as, the power of God in the wilderness.

THE DANGERS OF THE WILDERNESS

Through a series of miracles, God liberated Israel from slavery and set them on a journey to the land that He had marked out for them. Their initial steps after the deliverance were full of anticipation, hope and joy (Ex 15:11). It was spiritually speaking, the highest peak of their lives. Full of positive expectations, they set off for the land "flowing with milk and honey".

Soon however, the Israelites had their excitement dampened. Within days of their liberation, they were to realize to their shock and horror that before they could enter the land of Canaan, they needed to trespass the harsh wilderness. Indeed, their journey to the Promised Land could have taken only a few weeks. We however learn from Ex 13:17 that though the road through the Philistine country would have been shorter, God chose another route. God instead "redirected the people around by the desert road toward the Red Sea". The path God chose for His redeemed people towards the Promised Land was not the straight and short and direct highway. Instead, He chose a long, winding and treacherous wilderness. Why did God do that?

Every one of God's children faces this wilderness experience sometime in their lives. It is a period when God seems to stop doing big interventions on behalf of His children. The spiritual wilderness is a period when the believer is exposed to harsh and bitter experiences. That is what the children of Israel discovered soon after their liberation.

The Israelites encountered five categories of dangers in the wilderness that threatened to derail their inheritance of God's promise. They faced the dangers of death, deprivation, spiritual warfare, indiscipline and falling away. Even though the physical effect of each danger as they progressed reduced, the severity of the spiritual threat increased with each danger. Just like the typical wilderness experience of the immigrant, the problems started with what was physical and material and gradually deepened to involve their spiritual state until they backslid and fell into apostasy.

The Danger of Death

The first difficulty Israel faced was in relation to the Red Sea. Immediately after God led them towards the wilderness, they became hemmed in, with no human route of escape. Ahead of them was the expansive Red Sea, ready to swallow them alive. Behind them was Pharaoh's galloping soldiers, full of vengeance to destroy Israel. Where could they turn?

This danger was in effect the most serious physical danger that Israel was to encounter during their wilderness migration. And guess what, it occurred right at the beginning of the exodus! Their complaint that, "It would have been better for us to serve the Egyptians than to die in the desert" (Ex 14:12), is perhaps a natural human response when faced with the inescapable danger of premature death. And death indeed, is the symbolism that the Red Sea represents.

Why did God hem Israel in this way? Why did He lead them towards the Red Sea, when He knew that Pharaoh was going to change his mind and pursue Israel? We can give a number of answers to these questions. Firstly, death at the Red Sea was to serve as the final judgment of Egypt. Though Egypt had experienced ten devastating plagues, the country did not repent and turn to God. Instead Egypt persistently hardened its heart. Death in the Red Sea was therefore God's final plague on a rebellious nation.

In addition, God had to deal the Egyptian army a massive blow through which He would protect Israel. Despite the fact that various ecological disasters had ravaged Egypt, the nation's armies remained generally intact and ready to attack and destroy God's people while they migrated. If God's chosen ones were to survive and continue in their journey to inherit their possessions, God needed to eliminate this threat from Egypt's army.

The Red Sea incident was therefore designed by God to serve as the great divider—just as the darkness, the locust, the frogs, the ecological disasters and the death of the firstborn sons served as the divider between the saved and unsaved. God brought His people to the Red Sea, hemmed them in, so that through death God would judge Egypt. That was His agenda.

The Red Sea incident was also a baptism of Israel into God's Kingdom (1 Cor 10:1-2). In stepping into the dry riverbed, Israel symbolically died with Christ and came out on the other side as a new creation. God's purpose in bringing Israel to the Red Sea was to begin a new creation. His strategy was to begin the formation and inauguration of a new nation of holy priests of God—people who would spread His glorious name throughout the world.

This is why the Red Sea incident was paradoxically the least of the spiritual temptations that Israel faced in the wilderness. It is the kind of trial in which one cannot do anything but "Stand firm and you will see the deliverance the LORD" (Ex 14:14). The Red Sea incident belongs to the category of difficulty that requires calm assurance and confidence in the wisdom and strategy of God. "Stand firm and see God's deliverance", is the solution when faced with the sort of danger that gives you no way of escape.

The Dangers in Deprivation

The second danger in the wilderness was deprivation. Soon after their deliverance from death at the Red Sea, Israel was faced with the dangers in lack of food and drink. In Ex 16, the population of Israel, of well over two million, was faced with the challenge of feeding itself in the wilderness. Almost immediately after God provided them with manna and quail from heaven, the next problem in Ex 17 was the lack of water to drink. This is typical of the immigration experience. For, sooner or later, the immigrant's physical and material resources dry up. In due course, the immigrant will need some extra help with money and other material resources to survive in a strange land.

Though these difficulties of food, water, shelter and clothing are related to the physical aspects of wilderness existence, they are more severe in their spiritual significance than the Red Sea incident. For, unlike the Red Sea incident, where Israel had no way of escape; when it came to food and drink, there was a choice for Israel. Israel could choose between trusting God for provisions in the wilderness or of turning back into Egypt. They had a choice between abandoning the whole project and going back to Egypt or sticking with it and depending on Jehovah.

For several Christians, and like Jesus in the wilderness, the first and most frequent temptations they face have to do with their natural physical and material needs—the need to eat and drink, to be nourished, clothed and sheltered. These temptations may appear on the surface to be less demanding of our physical capital. They certainly do not endangering our lives in an imminent way. What they do however is to tax our spiritual resources in very severe manner.

And like Jesus in the wilderness, these dangers of deprivation offer us various choices of solutions. Behind them are the whispers of the serpent to turn these stones into bread! So the traps in these deprivations of material things are within the choices we make—whether we will choose God's way of providing us the money, food, shelter and clothing or we will choose other ways. Each day, the devil presents immigrants with short-cuts for meeting their deprivations, just as he did with Jesus in the wilderness.

The financial hardships that many immigrants face may not imminently threaten their physical lives. They are however very serious spiritual traps. Believers must therefore discern these traps and learn to live by every Word that comes from the mouth of the Lord. Just as God fed Israel in the wilderness, He will also feed believers if they will continue to trust and obey Him.

The Danger of Spiritual Warfare

The next challenge for Israel in the wilderness is recorded in Ex 17:8-16 and involved a mixture of physical and spiritual dangers. This was the war against the Amalekites. Israel had avoided the Philistines, and God had dealt with Egypt, but at some point, they had to fight some battle. Israel could not escape from the issue of fighting forever. At some point in his or her life, every child of God must deal with this issue of spiritual warfare. Every one of us believers must one day face up to the demonic attacks of the devil upon our loved ones.

This battle was not Israel's own choosing. They were attacked from the rear by Amalek. We know this encounter with the Amalekites was a spiritual battle because while Joshua fought against them in the plains, his victory did not depend on his fighting skills. On the contrary, Joshua's victory depended on the intercession that Moses and Aaron were conducting up there on the hill (Ex 17:11). Israel was being taught at this early stage of their walk with God in the wilderness that, "the weapons we fight with are not the weapons of the world" (2 Cor 10:4). Like Israel, our victory will begin only when we realize that the battle is only won up there on the mountain of intercession.

The Danger of Indiscipline

Most of the remaining dangers that Israel faced in the wilderness are recorded in the Book of Numbers. On the surface these dangers would appear to be little unimportant issues. In many other ways however, these little dangers kept chewing away the spiritual resources of Israel and in turn stirred God's anger against them. In Num 11, the people begun complaining and grumbling bitterly against God. This time, it was not because they were hungry. They complained bitterly because they were literally fed up with the heavenly food God gave them. They started craving for "the fish we ate in Egypt at no cost", the cucumbers, melons, leeks, onions and garlic.

With rose-tinted eyes, the Israelites began to hanker for the leftovers they had enjoyed as slaves in Egypt. In their carnality, God's heavenly food became despised and belittled in their eyes. They grumbled and protested about how they had lost their appetite because "we never see anything but *this* manna!" (Num 11:5–6, emphasis added).

Such language of ingratitude and dissatisfaction, which scorns at the "little" blessings of God, illustrates a lack of spiritual depth and humility. It demonstrates that the people's focus had moved on from God's provision onto envying, lusting after and craving for what belonged to others. That feeling of dissatisfaction with one's lot is the beginning of greed, and the source of grave temptations (James 1:14–15). The Israelites' inability to control these passions stimulated God's anger and led to divine discipline.

The nature of God's discipline in this case is very instructive. The bible says, God gave the Israelites their heart's cravings, but with it also came spiritual leanness. Due to the hot weather, the meat the Israelites received got infected and led to food poisoning in the camp. Several thousands died as a result. We never know how much trouble God is protecting us from in not answering some of our prayers!

Another series of dangers that are depicted in the Book of Numbers are recorded in Num 12, 16 & 21. They all amount to community indiscipline and rebellion against spiritual authority. In Num 12, Aaron and Miriam, out of jealousy, started bad-mouthing and backbiting against Moses. Sins of the tongue—lying, flattery, gossip, slander, boasting, obscenity, swearing and such like, destroy the fellowship of believers. Think of how many churches and families have been destroyed by the undisciplined tongue of one of its members.

In Num 16, a number of the junior priests of the congregation complained about the extraordinary influence and power of Moses. They were impatient for their turn to be leaders. Soon, they became dissatisfied with what they regarded as the lack of democracy in the things of God. What is clear from Num 21 is that people who repeatedly complain and agitate against spiritual authority sooner or later begin to rise up against God Himself. The impatience of these young priests eventually led to rebellion against the Lord. It is only a matter of time before the undisciplined disciple of Christ slips into apostasy and begins to hurl insults against the Lord Jesus who bought him.

The Danger of Falling Away

So the "little" indisciplines of Israel in the wilderness eventually resulted in turning their backs from the Lord and falling away into apostasy. All of the people, who migrated from Egypt, apart from two, forfeited the Promised Land.

Two incidents in the wilderness were particularly responsible. The first one was at the foot of Mount Sinai where Israel rejected God and made and worshipped the golden calf (Ex 32). The other occurred in the plains of Kadesh–Barnea when the spies brought an evil report that instigated rebellion among God's people (Num 13–14). These incidents, together with the general spiritual decay of the people, resulted in their excommunication from God's inheritance.

Israel

Israel fell in the wilderness through one sin—unbelief. It was their refusal to believe in God's love and kindness, and their refusal to submit to the agenda of Jehovah that led to their apostasy. Israel refused to believe that God brought them into the wilderness to bless them and not to destroy them. They began to search for substitutes and second bests.

Israel stopped believing that their God was bigger and stronger than the gods of the Canaanites and the gods of the heathen. And so they questioned God's wisdom and intentions. They refused to believe that God meant to lead them for good and not for evil. It was this unbelief that led to Israel's downfall in the wilderness. How many believers are falling preys to this sin of unbelief on a daily basis?

THE POWER OF GOD IN THE WILDERNESS

Looking at the many dangers in the wilderness and the sad end of the experiences of Israel, one may be right in asking, was there any benefit at all in going through the wilderness? Did God have His strategies right in leading them there? In the middle of their struggles, many immigrants also ask similar questions. What is God's purpose for the wilderness experience? Was the wilderness really necessary?

Molded in the Wilderness

The answer to these questions is simple—God's plan for Israel in the wilderness was for a good purpose. The wilderness was necessary so that God would fashion out a special people who could be His effective ambassadors to the world. This is precisely what He told them when they arrived at the foot of Mount Sinai. He told them that out of all nations, Israel would be His treasured possession. "Although the whole earth is mine", God told Israel, "you will be for me a kingdom of priests and a holy nation" (Ex 19:5-6).

God's strategy in bringing Israel into the barren desert was to carve this mob of undisciplined former slaves into a kingdom of holy priests who will bear His glorious name to all peoples of the earth. The preparation, training and molding of the people to qualify them to minister as channels of blessings, could only occur in the wilderness. That is why the wilderness was necessary.

Without the wilderness, Israel would not have been able to possess and keep their possession. Though harsh, the wilderness was necessary to bring out the full potential of the people of God. The wilderness holds great possibilities and blessings for the children of God. If only Israel knew in advance that the agenda of Jehovah in the harsh desert was to make a new people for Himself—people who would love Him and serve Him in full dedication and surrender, what a difference it would have made to their attitude while there in the wilderness.

The wilderness is a place of testing and proving the people of God. It is the place where God transforms our material and physical experiences into spiritual gold for the sake of His kingdom. After forty years in the wilderness, after all the dangers of death, deprivation, spiritual warfare, indiscipline and apostasy, Moses told Israel,

> "Remember how the LORD your God led you all the way in the desert these forty years; to humble you and to test you in order to know what was in your heart ... He humbled you, causing you to hunger and then feeding you with manna ... to teach you that man does not live on bread alone but on every word that comes from the mouth of the LORD. Your clothes did not wear out and your feet did not swell during these forty years. Know then in your heart that as a man disciplines his son, so the LORD your God disciplines you." Deut 8:2–5

Our wilderness experiences, as it was for Israel, prove that we are indeed God's children. It is the children He loves that He disciplines and prunes. Like His Son, who was led by the Holy Spirit into the wilderness to prove to the devil that the Lord God is indeed His loving Father who will never leave Him nor forsake Him, so are we to remain steadfast and immovable.

The wilderness is also the place to seek the fellowship of God's people against isolation and loneliness. It is the place to remain strengthened with love, forgiveness and affection for the people of God. The wilderness is the place to experience the covenantal nature of the relationship with God—to be bonded to fellow believers and to submit to the discipline of being part of the body of Christ.

The wilderness is the place to learn to eschew the lusts of the flesh. It is the place to learn personal discipline and self-control. The wilderness is the place to learn to be content with what we have. It is the place to learn how not to crave for the things that one cannot have. It is also the place to learn to be abased and humbled. It is the place to learn to accept the loving provisions of God, though they seem not to come in big heaps. The small mercies of our wilderness are indeed big blessings from our loving Father above. Cherish them.

The wilderness is also the place to watch and see the wonderful acts of power of God. When we are well fed, and have all the money, and good health, the house, car and loving family around us—when we are outside the wilderness, we don't feel that we need a miracle, and we don't see the powerful hand of God in our lives on a daily basis. It is only in the wilderness of difficulties that God comes closer to His children, intervenes on their behalf and performs mighty miracles for them. Our wilderness is the place to experience the power of God.

The wilderness is also the place to rekindle our first-love for Christ. As we go through the wilderness of hardship and confusion, I trust that one day we will look back and be grateful for God's kindness and provision during the time. Yes, the wilderness experience may now feel harsh and bitter, but it is there in the wilderness that we will see the display of the power and presence of God among His people.

God's Acts of Power in the Wilderness

Reflect specifically on the acts of power that Israel experienced in their wilderness. Firstly, they experienced God's extraordinary guidance in the wilderness. These freed slaves were going to a place they had never been before. Yet, Israel knew they will get there because their God was going to guide them. Right at the beginning of their exodus, God provided Israel the angel of His presence, with the pillar cloud by day and pillar of fire by night (Ex 13:21-22). Israel did not know, and did not always feel that the angel of God was before and behind them all the time through the wilderness (Ex 14:19). Yet, He was.

Like Israel, sometimes believers don't feel God's power in their wilderness because they stereotype and package Him. We expect Him to behave in a certain specific way all the time. Like Elijah in his wilderness, we want God to show His power through the wind and the storm and the earthquake. Yet God's power is also as active in His "still small voice". His power is released in the whispers and assurances and quiet energy that He gives us in our wilderness.

God sends His angels to minister to us who are bound to inherit His great salvation. These angels are all around us, like Jesus, to guard our feet from stumbling. Even in our confusion in the wilderness, not knowing which choice to make, afraid that we might get our decisions wrong, the Lord God provides His guidance for His children. God provides His extraordinary guidance even when we do not see it. We must just learn that He, who leads us into the wilderness, has not made a mistake and will not abandon us.

Another act of power by God in the wilderness was the covenant with Israel. God brought Israel right to the foot of Mount Sinai in order to enact a pact with them so that they would know how much He loved and cherished them. Why did He bring them into the wilderness for this? Because it is there in the wilderness that Israel, freed from all other commitments and distractions will also learn to devote herself wholly and fully to their God. Love and commitment is what a covenant is for.

The Bible says that in these last days, God has established a new covenant with the people He loves. This covenant is sealed with His own blood so that it is irrevocable. What this covenant does is to assure us—to make us "Know the Lord" and to make us know our true identity in Jesus (Jer 31:34). What this covenant does is to cut off the dross of Egypt and create a new heart within us. It is in the wilderness of our experiences that we know how close our God is to us, and how loved and cherished we are to Him. It is there that we can learn to grow closer to Him. God has a business to perform on your life in the wilderness. Let His Spirit do it.

Another act of power by God in the wilderness was the building of the tabernacle. This tabernacle was a symbol of the presence of God among His people. It contained the ark and the mercy seat, which was symbolic of the throne of God from where He reigns among His redeemed people. Each time Israel saw the ark, they knew that God was in control. Only in the wilderness was the tabernacle for real, so near and so tangible to the redeemed people of God. Moses was not telling Pharaoh fibs when he asked him to let Israel go into the wilderness to worship God. For truly, it was there in the wilderness that they came so near their God and worshipped Him!

The Bible tells God's children that, even now, we also have a high priest "who sat down at the right hand of the throne of the majesty in heaven" (Heb 8:1–2). In the wilderness of our hardships, the Lord Jesus who sits on the throne is our high priest who also intercedes on our behalf. He also receives and grants God's favor upon us. What a privilege and what a blessing to be in His very presence in our wilderness. That is

Israel

how and why as God's children, immigrants in this world, we can and will experience God's power in our wilderness.

DISCUSSION QUESTIONS

1. One of the most serious problems within the immigrant communities of the country is quarrelling, bickering and divisions. What lessons do the Exodus generation in the wilderness teach us about this particular problem?
2. Many new Christians struggle to understand how to go about making the right decisions in this world. From the examples of Israel's experience in the wilderness, what are some of the means by which they can receive guidance from God?
3. From Heb 8–9, what can we learn about the significance of the tabernacle of God to the Christian experience in this world?

Samson

How Can You Be Tied Up and Subdued: Why Some Immigrants Fail

NOT ALL IMMIGRANTS ARE as successful in their new environment as Abraham and Joseph were. Some end up as abysmal failures. In a minority of cases, failure is demonstrated by involvement in serious crime. It is true that despite the public perception, no doubt fuelled by sensational mass media headlines, there is no direct evidence to link immigration with increased crime. Indeed, the evidence suggests that foreign born immigrants commit fewer crimes compared to the native populations.

Nevertheless, it is a matter of extreme distress to most independent observers when an immigrant becomes involved in serious crime. As I write, there have been disturbing reports in the mass media, of shootings involving gangs of immigrant youth in London and Manchester. It makes one question what went wrong in the short life of a seventeen year old Angolan immigrant to take up arms, and kill two innocent women within a fortnight. One of these women was cradling a baby at a Christening party when she was killed. This boy, who came to UK as a refugee from the Angolan civil war, has clearly and disastrously failed. One would least have expected such a person to commit such a crime.

Indeed there are increasingly bleak reports that suggest a worrying trend of failure and descent into drugs, prostitution and violence emerging among some immigrant populations in Europe and America. These developments feed into historical perceptions of organized crimes by immigrants, such as those by the Russian, South American or Italian Mafias in a number of US cities decades ago. The recent increase of religious extremism and terrorism only serves to concretize the perception of linkage between violent crime and immigration. It is hence becoming difficult to shake away the popular myth that links immigration with serious crimes.

Indeed, in some cases, the facts are worrying. For instance, although Afro-Caribbean males constitute only one percent of UK's population; there is the distressing fact that they account for ninety percent of the gun crime and twenty five percent of all robberies in the UK. Some of these offenders are immigrants or come from immigrant families. There is no need to excuse these statistics which represent a grave failure in that sub-section of the immigrant community. One cannot therefore be complacent with regard to immigration and crime. Every crime committed by an immigrant is a disastrous failure.

In other areas apart from crime, the link between immigration and social failure cannot be disputed. In a 1997 report to the European Parliament, for example, Prof D. M. Morina, Principal Administrator of the Union's Division for Policies on Social Affairs, Women, Health and Culture, highlighted that unemployment among immigrants who have moved from third world countries to Europe is as high as three times that of natives. The major reason for this massive discrepancy is educational failure. Prof Morina notes, "Failure at school, heralding lack of success in society, only reinforces the inferior status which immigrants are often perceived as having"[1].

The statistics are even more worrying in the US. The poverty rate among immigrants in the US as at 1998 was fifty percent higher than among natives. According to Steven A. Camarota, the major reason for this difference again is educational failure—thirty one percent of high school dropouts, who then constitute a large proportion of the unskilled labor market, are immigrants. This discrepancy is not universally true for all immigrant populations however. For, whereas the rate of poverty among British immigrants to the US in 1998 was only eight percent, and among Indian immigrants was even lower at six percent; that among Mexicans was thirty one percent[2].

It may be rightly argued that the failure depicted here is only a reflection of the financially poor backgrounds of legal or illegal immigrants.

1. D. M. Morina, Report on the Teaching of Immigrants in the European Union, 1997. Accessed @ http//www.europarl.europa.eu/workingpapers/educ/pdf/100_en.pdf, 2/10/07.

2. See article by Stephen Camarota @ http://www.ci.org/articles/1999/back199.html accessed 2/20/07.

Because they have inadequate education, skills and legal residency status, some immigrants are unable to secure good jobs and the financial abilities to educate their children. Even among those who may have legal residency, not a few immigrants are exposed to discrimination and racism. Some are denied employment or are employed in jobs far below their qualifications. Others are paid wages far below those of their native counterparts of similar qualifications and job descriptions. It is true that the failure of some immigrants cannot be totally blamed on them alone. For some, it is the system that fails them.

Notwithstanding the above caveat, a most serious component to the failure of some immigrants occurs, now and again, in families that are not as deprived. These are immigrant youth who have been exposed to as good educational opportunities as could be had by the natives. And yet, who slide gradually or even sometimes in a short period of months into an identity crisis and social deviance.

These are young people whose parents have already done all the struggling against deprivation and discrimination. Their parents have, despite the odds, managed to endure the harshness and made something of themselves. And yet, despite these efforts, their children have grown up to gradually reject this heritage. They have instead slipped into callous living, laziness, bad company and eventually into criminality.

What causes the failure of promising youth, of talented and well-educated children with the whole world potentially at their feet? What went wrong with youth who grew up with excellent prospects to make something of themselves, avoid the poverty trap of their parents, and change their society? Instead, they have ended up big failures, now dependent on the society to rehabilitate them?

Samson, whose brief life history is narrated in Judges 13–16, was one such example of an immigrant who turned out to be a failure. Born through miraculous revelations, with great promise and natural talent, Samson turned out to be undisciplined, violent and a stark failure. All his great gifts and prospects were squandered in a man who could not control his appetites. Samson's life teaches us lessons on why some immigrants don't succeed despite the vast opportunities they may have.

To start with, it has to be clarified that Samson was not a typical immigrant. His parents hailed from Zorah in the western Israelite region of Dan, which was the borderland north of the Philistines. For all of Samson's life however, this land was under the control of the Philistines.

Infact, according to Josh 19:47, the Danites were unable to fully subdue the land allotted to them by Joshua. They were almost always ruled by the Philistines until the time of Hezekiah several centuries later. Hence the Danites were regarded by the Philistines as immigrants. Certainly, Samson and his parents spent their lives more or less as colonized people in their own land.

In addition, all of Samson's exploits occurred among the cities and countryside of the Philistines, in Timnah, Ashkelon, Gaza and Sorek. At another time he was an asylum seeker in Judah, running away from the mischief that he had caused to the Philistines. Samson was therefore as displaced a person as any immigrant, an alien in his environment. There is therefore much to learn from Samson on how to fail as an immigrant, and an alien of God's kingdom. The story of Samson in Judg 13–16 neatly divides itself in three parts—the promise of Samson, the failure of Samson and the revival of Samson.

THE PROMISE OF SAMSON

From the point of view of the Bible, there are very few people who, at their births, had more potential than Samson. Judges 13 creates a very high expectation that in itself seems destined for an anticlimax. An examination of the details of Samson's early life also reveals interesting parallels with Christian discipleship.

First of all, Samson had a special and miraculous birth. We are told that his mother was barren. Like the stories of Sarah who gave birth to Isaac, and Rachel who gave birth to Joseph, and Hannah who gave birth to Samuel, and Elizabeth who gave birth to John the Baptist; the Bible prepares us for a great man to be born. Samson also shared with only three other bible characters the special privilege of his birth being announced in advance of his conception by an angel of the Lord. The others were Isaac, John the Baptist and the Lord Jesus. Clearly, God was heavily investing into the life of Samson.

Every believer shares with Samson the same privilege of a special and miraculous birth. All believers were chosen "before the creation of the world to be holy and blameless" as God's adopted children (Eph 1:4–5). That is why Christians are as privileged as Samson. We are men or women of promise, people bought, not with silver or gold but with the blood of the Lamb of God. Believers were destined before the foundations of the world to be Christ's change agents in this world.

Secondly, Samson was destined for a special calling. He was marked out before birth to be dedicated to God for a specific mission. The angel told his mother that the child would be a Nazirite—"set apart to God from birth" (Judges 13:5). The Nazirite custom was instituted by Moses in Num 6 for any person in Israel who so wished, to completely dedicate a period of his or her life to the service of God. During that period, the Nazir abstained from wine or fermented drink, no contact with any corpse and not shaving the hair. This vow was always made for a limited period of the person's life, usually a few months, as was the case of Paul in Acts 18. As Amos 2:11–12 notes, the Nazirite vow was a demonstration of the extraordinary devotion and self-control of Israel's young people. It was one means by which they demonstrated how different they were from the other nations of the world.

Samson was set apart before he was born to become such a person. His vow however, was more than just a temporary one. Samson's period of dedication and separation to God was not limited to a short period, not to a few months or years. His separation was for the whole of his life. This illustrates how special Samson was, for he became the only permanent Nazirite in the Bible.

Besides, Samson's vow was involuntary. For, Samson was conscripted by God before his birth. Throughout his life, he was to walk, not as belonging to himself but as a person who was marked out by God as His special agent in the world. What an extraordinary responsibility was being invested by God in this one man?

In addition to being a Nazirite, Samson was also called to fulfill an important mission. The angel told his mother that Samson "will *begin* the deliverance of Israel" (Judges 13:5, emphasis added). Samson's mission was to begin something great on behalf of the kingdom of God. He was to be the starting point, the instigator and the commencement of the deliverance of Israel. There are some people who believe they are born to continue projects, businesses, and family traditions. They do not bring new ideas or any new revolution to their environment. They merely keep the status quo and traditional way of doing things. Samson was not like that. Instead, he was to begin a new thing for God and His people.

Like Samson, every one of us believers is called to begin something for the sake of the kingdom of God. The redemption of our families, friends, and colleagues begin with us. The revival of our churches, the transformation of our neighborhoods, and the restoration of the backslidden Christian begin with men and women who will set their hearts to obey Christ and serve Him in their small corners.

Some believers are called by God to complete what others have started. Theirs is to build on other people's foundations. They are to ensure that the gains of the kingdom are brought to fruition and that God is glorified. Jesus told his disciples—"One sows and another reaps" (Jn 4:37). This is the nature of the calling for many Christians—to bring to completion the hard work that others have started.

Each and every Christian has a special calling—whether to begin something, restore something, ensure that something grows to fruition or to harvest something. We are not in this world for nothing. We have been bought by the precious blood of Christ to fulfill a mission. This mission, like Samson's, was marked out on us before we became embryos in our mothers' wombs. God told Jeremiah, that before he was formed in his mother's womb, he was set apart and appointed "as a prophet to the nations" (Jer 1:5). And that is what we are—prophets to the nations.

Samson was more than just a finisher of other people's work, or a preserver of what others had started. Samson was meant to be a pioneer, a pathfinder and path breaker. He was a special apostle of God to begin the deliverance of God's people from the dark oppression of the Philistines.

Many Christian immigrants find themselves in a similar situation—as pioneers and pathfinders. They are beginning things that no one from their families or even cities has ever done before. Samson's responsibilities and privileges were immense and so are these immigrants. These Christian immigrants may be in schools or businesses where no one has ever talked publicly about Christ or even worshipped him with confidence. They may be in churches where no one has dared to think or pray for revival and God's anointing on His congregation. Perhaps their calling is to begin something, to start and instigate the movement of God where they are. Believers are God's Samson, aliens of the kingdom sent into their present environments for its expansion.

Thirdly, Samson was a man of promise because of the special gifts and talents he had. Of course God never sends His servants on a mission without giving them the prerequisite gifts and enablement to help them fulfill the assignment. And Samson was like that. We are told that as he grew, "the Spirit of the LORD began to stir him" (Judges 13:25). And that is always the secret of success in God's service. It was through the power of the Spirit of God that Samson could begin to fulfill his mission.

The ministry that is not based on a "stirring" of God's Spirit like Samson's is bound to yield rubble and chaff—it will eventually fail (Acts 1:8). And this is not just to do with preaching or leading a church. Each and every work that God has given us, whether in the raising up of children or in the Christian testimony we present at our work or in our mundane business—without the Spirit of God upon us, we will have no power and no lasting results. Samson was privileged in having that gift.

It was not just the gift of the Spirit of God that Samson had. He also had physical strength as a special talent that God gave him. Added to this was the immense privilege in having a God fearing mother. This great woman of God, though unnamed, comes across throughout the story as calm, confident and in control of the household. Unlike her husband, she was devoted to God and believed the Word of God with calmness. Samson was very privileged to have had a mother like her.

Samson was also a very intelligent man. Some Bible readers imagine that Samson was an idiotic and violent rogue who delighted in causing mischief. That is far from the truth. A careful study of his riddles, and the way he went about bantering with his Philistine friends at the wedding, suggests that he was a very knowledgeable person. He knew how to play on words and create difficult puns and riddles for his enemies. Though he chose to live foolishly, Samson was no fool. Many believers are as blessed as Samson was. Are we like Samson, going to squander such great promise and waste it?

THE FAILURE OF SAMSON

Despite his great promise and his excellent prospects, we the readers of Samson's biography cannot but feel disappointed by his overall achievement in life. He himself felt disappointed. His prayer at the end of his life summarizes it all. He prayed to God "Let me die with the Philistines" (Judges 16:30). At the end of his career, Samson merely wanted to die with the same people that he so detested. These were the people he had, in his hey days, called "uncircumcised" (Judges 15:18).

This outcome of Samson's mission was completely opposite to what Paul, his New Testament counterpart could say. Also at the end of his life, Paul declared, "I have fought the good fight". Samson could not say that. With his eyes gorged out, the disgraced strong man of Israel, we are told, could only plead with a "young lad" to help him feel the pillars of the banquet hall! What a miserable end to a career that started before his birth with an announcement by an angel?

Even more depressingly, we read this about Samson at the end of his career—"he did not know that the LORD had left him" (Judges 16:20). It is a very severe outcome for the Spirit of God to abandon His agent. Only one other person in the Bible has been described in such terms, and he was King Saul, the son of Kish. What is really serious about these two was not just that the Spirit of God had left them. What was more serious was the fact that they did not know that this had happened to them. It is a wretched situation in the life of a child of God, to sink so low in the estimation of the Lord, and yet not aware that this exactly is what has happened.

There may be some of God's children today who sadly find themselves in a similar situation. There are some Christian immigrants who started off full of hope and expectations of being ambassadors for Christ in their environment. Yet, they now have their testimony dimmed, their fervency cut off, their power smothered and their witness damaged. What went wrong with them? What caused the failure of Samson?

Samson's failure stemmed from failure in four areas in his life—the failures of the community, the family, friendship and personal discipline. First of all, Samson's failure was partly due to the failure of his community. He grew up in the period of the Judges that was marked by social confusion, community breakdown, anarchy and the failure of law and order. Without a strong central government, with the loss of spiritual giants like Joshua and Caleb, and with the clamor after material wealth and fame in the country, this period is rightly regarded by many as the dark ages of Israel's history.

The Bible repeatedly describes the period of the judges this way—"everyone did as he saw fit" (Judges 17:6, 18:1, 19:1 & 21:25). Because they had no strong leadership and identity as a people of God, Israel slipped into pursuing other kinds of identities to fill the void. They forgot about their God-given mission to transform the region into the citadel for the worship of Jehovah. They instead turned themselves to copying the idol worship and the paganism and the syncretic religions of the Canaanites.

Economically and socially, the country was afflicted by frequent raids and colonization by foreign powers. This resulted in instability and lack of social cohesion. The various tribes of Israel ceased to care for each other and rather sought to concentrate on their own survival. A typical example is in the way the people of Judah handed Samson over to the Philistines when he sought for asylum with them in Judges 15. They lived in so much fear that they didn't care for each other.

The problem with the community within which Samson grew was not primarily economic, political or even social. The problem with that community was primarily spiritual and theological. Judges 2:10 accurately assesses the root of the problem with that society. The writer says, "Another generation grew up, who knew neither the LORD nor what he had done for Israel" (Judges 2:10). It was not enough that the generation did not know the Lord. It also didn't know about God's involvement in the past history of the nation!

This description has a ring of post-modernity to it. It portrays a generation today that wishes to wipe out the Ten Commandments from its courts, erase the name of God from its pledges and abolish the teaching of the things about God that its founding fathers believed. Samson's society is surely similar to some countries today. Only a few centuries ago these countries sent out Christian missionaries to all over the world. Now the same countries are even ashamed of such a proud history. Instead, they have slumped into a lack of spiritual confidence and confusion about their own past dealings with God. Samson's society was very much like ours.

The people of Samson's community, according to Judges 13:1 had again done evil in the sight of God. He had consequently turned them over unto servitude under the Philistines for forty years. This was a repetition of the cycle of disobedience leading to punishment and then failure and distress described so well in Judges. The message of the book of Judges is this: "Righteousness exalts a nation, but sin is a disgrace to any people" (Prov 14:34).

Samson lived in an environment in which sin was a natural way of life. And so he reaped its disgrace. He was a product of the spiritual and theological failure of his community. When young people with great promise fail, we should ask ourselves whether the failure is not, as it was in the case of Samson, also due to the failure of our communities.

Samson's failure was secondly due to his family. Failure of many immigrants is not infrequently traceable to a problem in their homes. We have already commented on the blessings that Samson's God-fearing mother brought to his life. Throughout the story on the other hand, Samson's father comes across not as spiritually astute as his wife. Where was he when the angel visited the first time? Perhaps he was on a legitimate business on the farm. However, where was he again when the angel visited his wife the second time on the farm in Judges 13:9? This man appears to be an absentee father.

Manoah's skepticism and unbelief may also be criticized. His demand for signs of proof of the veracity of the angel's words suggests that he was a man, who though was ready to believe God, would only do so on his own terms and not God's. We have to praise Manoah for his prayerfulness, and his willingness to be led by his godly wife and to accept God's blessings through his wife. There are a number of Christian families like that in which, but for the faith and commitment of the wife, there would have been no spiritual progress. Despite these good qualities, Manoah does not meet the high standards of spiritual headship expected of him.

The family also failed to rein in and discipline Samson in the matter of his marriage to a Philistine woman and in his selection of questionable friends. The writer of Judges tells us that Samson's parents tried to dissuade him from his course of action and failed. They perhaps felt torn in two—whether to reject their son or to resign themselves to a marriage that was a second best. They chose the latter option, not knowing, as the bible warns us, that God was going to use it in the end for His own purposes. Samson's parents resigned themselves to their son's hardheadedness and said, "There is nothing we can do any more. The boy has set his heart on doing the wrong thing and we are being emotionally blackmailed to either give in or lose him". Faced with such an impossible choice, Samson's parents gave in.

In many parts of the world today, Christian parents are being emotionally blackmailed on a daily basis and in similar fashion. They are being faced with children who "know their rights", insist on them and refuse to budge to please their parents. What should these parents do? Should they give in and make their children "happy"? Or should they insist on their children's "obedience" and risk alienating them? Faced with such emotional blackmail, many, like Samson's parents, give in to the second best.

The Bible presents the story of the failure of Samson's family without appearing to judge it because it wants us to deeply reflect on how a society like Samson's could come to be like this. Ours is to ponder on the whole failure of the family unit in this story. How did it come to be like this? What causes such a situation when the instructions, advice and warnings of godly parents become inadequate to shape the characters and choices of their young people? What is the future for such a society?

We know there was failure in Samson's family, not only because of the issue of his interest in women of questionable backgrounds. There was also failure with regard to his parents' participation in his indiscretions. The writer of the Book of Judges leaves us with clues all over the story about how this family, which, to several outsiders appeared normal, was however bereft of cohesion in its internal workings. Apart from his parents giving their approval to the doomed marriage, notice how Samson kills a lion, and in order to make sure we don't miss the point, the Bible states that Samson did not tell his parents about it.

One would have thought that killing a lion was not Samson's daily routine. So why did he not tell his parents? The Bible leaves us wondering what the nature of the relationship within this family unit was like. Samson's confession to his Timnite wife in Judges 14:16, that he had not explained his riddle "even to my father or mother", is meant by the author of Judges, to highlight this lack of communication.

The absence of honest and open communication is one major cause and symptom of family failure and it is written all over this story. So again, when Samson broke one of his vows, ate the honey from the corpse of the lion and gave some to his parents, the writer tells us again that he did not tell his parents where he got it from. And they didn't ask him the source either (Judg 14:6, 9). The hint the writer is giving is that there was a failure of effective, open and honest communication within Samson's family.

Several families fail because of this lack of communication. The lack of "eyeball to eyeball" type of talk between family members so that everybody knew what was going on in the other's life, is one major cause of family failure. Churches fail when Christians hide behind jargons and clichés and refuse to share their struggles and exploits with each other. Marriages fail when husbands and wives bottle up and withdraw in coldness from each other. Samson's failure was a symptom of the failure of the family unit of his time.

There is more evidence of this failure of the family unit in the whole of the Book of Judges. The Israelites, we are told in Judges 3:5–6 "took the daughters [of the Canaanites] in marriage and gave their own daughters to their sons, and served their gods". Samson was therefore, following the fashion. And when that happens, the result is the failure of the family structure. The breakdown and divisions of Gideon's marriage and family in Judges 6–8 is another evidence of this family upheaval in the Book of Judges. So also is the chaos and bloodshed in Abimelech's family (Judges 9:23–24). Several of such examples of the failure of the family are dotted throughout the Book of Judges. When the family unit is struggling to flourish, its young promising youth will also struggle to fulfill their God-given missions in the world. That contributed to Samson's downfall.

Samson was terrible, not only with regard to friendship with women. He also had a very bad taste in his choice of friends. When it came to courting and marriage, Samson could not just resist the Timnite woman he saw down in the valleys of the Philistines. When that marriage failed, the next woman in his life was a prostitute in the Philistine city of Gaza. And then later on, he again went in to Delilah. Samson's lack of insight and carefulness in his choice of female companions also extended to male friends. This inability to discern the good from the bad in the matter of company was a major contributor to Samson's problems.

The story of Samson illustrates also how the failure of self-discipline may lead to the downfall of a person of promise. For a man who was dedicated to God to live a life of discipline, Samson again and again failed to measure up to the expectations of his office. The vows that were made on his behalf only appear to have served as an invitation for him to flout every one of them. First was his inability to control his sexual appetite. In choosing women whose characters were directly opposite to his mother's, was Samson deliberately rejecting such moral examples? Soon, Samson went in after a prostitute in Gaza. And then there was Delilah, a woman, who at every turn used and manipulated Samson's affections in order to earn some money.

It is fascinating that when lust takes control, the eyes can be so blind. It is therefore ironic that the Philistines gorged out Samson's eyes when they arrested him? Were they trying to tell him that "if your eye causes you to sin, pluck it out. It is better for you to enter the kingdom of God with one eye than to have two eyes and be thrown into hell" (Mk 9:47)?

Samson also struggled to control his physical appetite, otherwise; he would not have broken his vows in eating from the lion's carcass. On another occasion when he was thirsty, Samson dared even to rebuke God (Judges 14:18). He also had difficulty in controlling his temper (Judg 14:19). Throughout the four chapters, his tantrums and violence expose a person who had no self-control. Samson was a vengeful person, who could not tolerate being cheated or his wishes refused. He was a man who liked to "get even" with his enemies (Judges 15:3). Even at his death Samson was concerned about vengeance on his enemies (Judges 16:28). This lack of self-discipline was one source of his downfall.

Samson could capture and kill a lion but he couldn't control his temper. He had the gifts and talents to enable him fulfill his God-given mission. He had the charm and charisma to captivate and impress people. Samson however lacked the fruit of the Spirit that comes with the work of the Spirit. Samson was gifted but he was not "fruited".

And isn't this one of the major problems we observe in some of our churches today. There are men and women who are gifted singers, talented instrumentalists, able actors, anointed preachers, exceptional teachers and even great pastors. There are several Christian brothers and sisters who are exceptionally gifted in ministry. And yet when it comes to the "small" matter of the fruit of the Spirit, they are lacking. They lack the love, the patience, the gentleness and the self-control that the Spirit brings into such lives. That was what happened to Samson.

THE REVIVAL OF SAMSON

The story of Samson ends on a sad but not completely bleak note. For, after all the mess in his life, Samson managed to fulfill part of his mission. Samson's calling, we must remember, was to *begin* the deliverance of Israel from the hands of the Philistines. In that respect, Samson dealt some blow to the oppressors of Israel when he died (Judges 16:27). One wonders how much he could have achieved if he had avoided the above failures.

Samson's death was infamous. He lived by violence and died by violence. He died a desperately lonely and disgraced servant of God, and in his enemy's hands. His body was left on the field to be later retrieved by his kinsmen whose company he had shunned during his lifetime.

Though all these are true, Samson also served part of his purpose when he died. That speaks volumes about how God brings turn-arounds and revival in any repentant person. Like the thief on the cross, Samson's death demonstrates that God will listen to the prayer of any person, even at the gates of hell. There are important lessons to be learnt in this.

Samson's brief pre-mortem revival depended on prayer. In his prayer, Samson admitted his disgrace and failures (Judges 16:28). He remembered the sovereignty of God when all hope was lost. He recognized that despite all his failings, His God was completely elevated above the bitterness and pettiness that human beings usually have. Human beings would have told Samson, "You have exhausted all the chances to change things. You have lost the opportunity. There are no more chances for you". God however, is not like that. God does not think in terms of human justice.

Samson threw himself upon God's sovereign grace and got His mercy. And that is how revival starts among God's people. When Jehovah is lifted high up in His congregation, people cease to walk by their petty rules and live by God's grace. They stop thinking that they have managed to figure God out in a neat package—what He does and does not do and so forth. Instead they begin to throw themselves in desperation at His mercy.

Samson's revival also depended on remembrance—God's remembrance and his own remembrance. He prayed to God, "Remember me". That is exactly what the thief on the cross asked of Jesus (Lk 23:42). "Remember me" is not a request for God to remember Samson's past exploits. It was a request for God to have grace and mercy on him. "Remember me" is a return to God's purposes and plans for His servant. It was a call upon God to work things out so that it came back to suit the original purpose of his calling.

Samson was also implicitly remembering the whole purpose of his life—his mission, and calling to *begin* the deliverance of Israel. Remember me was therefore a return to the angel's words to his mother. It was a return to the plan for which God elected this young man.

That is similar to what Jesus told a group of Christians in the first century who were failing in their mission. This church used to be mission oriented and committed to the agenda of Christ in its environment. For some reasons it had fallen into spiritual confusion and lack of focus. It then became lukewarm and lost its first love for Jesus. For their revival, Jesus told them "Remember the height from which you have fallen. Repent and do the things you did at first" (Rev 2:5). Remember, repent and return to your first love. That was Jesus' message to the Church of Ephesus. And that is the exact message to any Christian, immigrant or not, who has failed in their discipleship—Remember, Repent and Return.

The revival of Samson also teaches something important about God's response to prayer. Biblical scholars have struggled to come up with a single theme for the Samson narrative in Judges 13–16. Some have suggested that the theme of vows and their fulfillment should guide its interpretation. Others think the complex nature of human failure and God's sovereignty is one theme. Still for others, it is the focus on how

Christian young men and women should handle themselves in a world that is dominated by the pursuit of pleasure.

To these, we must also add the theme of answered prayer. Notice for example, how from the beginning God promptly answers the prayers, even some of the "unreasonable" prayers of Manoah and his wife. Then Samson's prayers are all answered, even when his motives are not completely attractive. That is how revival happens. It happens only when we get on our knees and pray and plead with God on behalf of ourselves and others. God will answer our prayers when we call on Him, even at the last minute and in desperation.

DISCUSSION QUESTIONS

1. Supposing you were Samson's parent when he insisted on marrying the Philistine woman despite your protests, what would you have done?
2. What do you think are the important causes of failure among the youth in your area? What should the church do about it?
3. Under what circumstances would God refuse to answer the prayer of a backslidden Christian?

Ruth

Your People Will Be My People:
Integrating Successfully in a Foreign Land

MANY BIBLE READERS ARE rightly surprised when they learn that the heart warming story of Ruth occurred during the same generation as Samson's. While the charismatic man of God was following prostitutes in the Red Light district of Gaza, a young Moabite woman was moving in the opposite direction. Ruth came to find faith in Jehovah, integrate herself under the wings of God's people and so became the great grandmother of King David and an ancestor of the Messiah. The Book of Ruth teaches that we should not despair even when faithfulness to God is hard to come by. For, there will still be a faithful remnant, somewhere in a small corner, in a small church or community, who will continue to be devoted to the Lord.

The story of Ruth is an immigration story all right but it works in the opposite direction to those of Abraham, Joseph and Samson. In Ruth, the immigrant is not an Israelite but a Moabite, who comes to believe in the God of Israel. She then migrates to Bethlehem out of commitment to her mother-in-law and her God. She works her way up, successfully integrates into her new environment and so becomes the woman of blessing to her new people.

Unlike a failed Samson, Ruth negotiated all the possible obstacles to her progress through a combination of her unwavering faith and commitment, humility, hard work and her willingness to be discipled and directed. She therefore comes out in the end as a blessing to all generations. God recognized Ruth's faithfulness, and inserts her name in the genealogy of the Lord Jesus in Matthew 1:5.

There are two broad aspects of the story of Ruth that are relevant to immigration. First of all there is the issue of returning home when immigration has failed. Then also the question of what the best ways of integrating immigrants in a foreign land are.

RETURNING HOME

The story of Ruth begins with the migration of an Israelite and his family to Moab. Elimelech's immigration was purely for economic reasons. There was famine in Judah and he needed to look after his family. To make matters worse, the two boys who were born to Elimelech and Naomi were chronically unwell. Mahlon's name means "sickness" and the other, Kilion, means "consumption". These two, probably had a congenital disease that made them weaklings. It may have been in consideration of the poor health of their children that Elimelech and Naomi felt they couldn't survive the famine and so immigrated to greener pastures. The decision therefore makes good economic sense.

Little did Elimelech and Naomi know that the end result would be more disastrous? They found out the hard way that the grass was not as green on the other side as it appeared. Within a period of ten years, Elimelech died, followed soon by the deaths of his two weak sons, leaving behind the three widowed women. Widowed and in a foreign land, what should Naomi do with her situation?

If we remember that the culture of both Israel and Moab at the time had no place for women, let alone widowed or unmarried women, Naomi's situation was very much cruel indeed. She left Bethlehem, which means "the house of bread", full of optimism and positive expectation. Now, only ten years later, Naomi has lost everything that she had. She was understandably very much distressed by her circumstances. Who wouldn't?

Similar depressing situations occur today. It is not uncommon to hear stories about immigrant women who have become widowed or single mothers in a strange land. They are unexpectedly faced with poverty and isolation in a foreign land. There are several immigrants whose social and economic circumstances have become worse than what they enjoyed back home. They migrated in order to seek for a better future for themselves and their families. Instead they are confronted with one tragedy upon another. How should they deal with their situation? Should they return home?

Ruth

A Difficult Decision

In Naomi's case, her decision to return home was made a little bit easier by the news that Bethlehem had once again become "the house of bread" (Ruth 1:6). The famine, from which Elimelech and Naomi were running, had now been replaced by abundant food and blessings. It was perhaps therefore, not so difficult for Naomi to decide to return home.

On the other hand, the decision could still have been a difficult one for Naomi. She could have worried about nasty comments from her countrymen and women when she returned. They surely would have commented about her failed decisions and tainted dealings with the Moabites. Naomi could have reasoned to herself that she had indeed burnt her bridges behind her and so there was no point returning home.

Or Naomi could have, out of self-pity and bitterness, cut herself off the new opportunities in Israel. Also, she could have been ashamed about her decision to migrate in the first place. So despite the good news that Bethlehem was now flourishing again, it could still have been a rather difficult decision for Naomi to go back home. In the end, Naomi wisely decided to swallow her pride, accept the failed migration and just return to Bethlehem to start afresh.

Several immigrants have been confronted with similar decisions about what to do next when things have not gone as they had expected. At some points in their lives, a number have concluded that all their hopes and expectations with which they first migrated have evaporated. Instead, what they are faced with is a constant battle of failure, misery, isolation and depression. Life in their foreign environment only serves to persistently remind them of what they could have been but have emphatically not achieved. In its place, while they continue to struggle, they repetitively hear of how their former counterparts back home have moved on in life. Their former colleagues have succeeded to make a better life for themselves and are richer, happier and more at peace.

What should these immigrants, when faced with a continuous depression and reminders of failure do? Should they throw in the towel, take the little money that they have earned, swallow their pride and go back home to start life all over again? Or should they wait, be patient, keep working hard, keep praying and trusting God and hope for their future "breakthroughs"? Which decision is the best one when confronted with a situation like Naomi's?

Clearly, there is no single answer to such a dilemma. Everyone, faced with such a situation will have to seek God's face for what His will is for them. For some people, the action of Naomi in returning home would be the most appropriate. For others however, returning home could be the beginning of another set of serious problems. For, when Naomi returned home, she did not stop struggling. She was partially right when she told her daughters-in-law in simple terms that they were only going to end up as burdens on her in Israel.

Indeed, it appears that Naomi was never completely happy when she returned home. Certainly, there is something sad about how the Bible portrays Naomi's character in the rest of the Book of Ruth. An illustration of this is her manner at the christening ceremony of Obed in Ruth 4. Although we should not make too much of what the Bible does not specifically describe, it is instructive that Naomi is silent throughout the ceremony.

The fact that the women needed to remind Naomi that Ruth loved her and was worth more than seven sons (Ruth 4:15), would suggest that despite the change in her circumstances, her joy was not full. She was back home with her own people and kindred and now had a grandson to sustain her husband's name. Yet, there is the persistently gloomy atmosphere in the Book of Ruth about Naomi. She must have felt that something irreplaceable has been snatched out of her for the rest of her life.

More on Naomi's attitude shortly, but for now, what we want to emphasize is that "returning home" is easier said than done. For some, their experience on returning home can be as bitter as their experience of remaining as immigrants in a strange land. This is why for some returnees who are able to migrate again, it is not long before they do so.

Perhaps they thought that returning home was better than being a stranger elsewhere. They are soon astonished to realize however, that when they returned home, they are still treated like strangers in their own country. They become conscious of the fact that within the period that they have been away, "home" has moved on. This is why readjusting to the situation of failed immigration has spelt the psychological and emotional destruction of not a few people. Returning home is much easier said than done.

Faced with the situation like Naomi's, not everyone will therefore decide to do what she did. It is a difficult decision. The choice is hence a balancing act between the misery of being an immigrant on the one hand, and the fear of the unknown but possible misery that awaits the immigrant on returning home. What one does is dependent on prayerful consideration and loving counsel from loved ones.

A Blinkered Vision

So Naomi decided to return and proposed to her two daughters-in-law to also go back to their parents and look for new husbands. Was Naomi's decision to dispense with her daughters-in-law right? They clearly wished to migrate with her to Bethlehem. And since she had a good relationship with them, why didn't she want to take them along with her?

It is obvious that Naomi's attempt to dispense with her daughters-in-law was not due to her concern for them. Otherwise she would not have been so desperate to insist on their return. On the contrary, and despite her religious clichés to the women, Naomi's intense efforts was a self-serving attempt to get rid of these women.

Naomi may have felt that Ruth was going to stigmatize her in Judah when they returned. She may have thought that her chances of putting her bitter past behind her were very slim so long as Ruth was strung around her neck. It therefore appears that in her bitterness, Naomi begun to regard these young women as difficult loads to carry along. In effect that is what her repeated attempts to dissuade them from following her meant.

Regardless of the pious religious language with which Naomi couched her words, her intense attempts at dissuading Ruth from following her were for Naomi's own sake. In her bitterness, Naomi even suggested that Ruth could go back to idol worship (Ruth 1:15). In this part of the story, Naomi, the discipler of the new believer, had become rigid and narrow minded in her vision. Instead of regarding these women as people to be drawn into God's kingdom, even perhaps as "trophies" she could have presented as the fruit of her ten years labor on the "mission field", Naomi looked upon Ruth as a burden and a difficult problem to handle.

That is what was happening in the tense exchanges between Ruth, the enthusiastic new believer and Naomi, the battered and bruised discipler. Here we meet Naomi's first failure as an alien of God's kingdom in a foreign land. Naomi should have perceived her ten years sojourn in Moab as a mission from God. Like Joseph, she should have recognized that she was where she was in relation to a specific agenda to do with God's kingdom. Naomi should have discerned that in Ruth, she had an opportunity to turn an unbeliever into a giant for God. Instead, in her disappointment, Naomi was attempting to throw away the baby with the bath water!

We all sometimes fall prey to this sort of failure. When many believers are faced with hardship and disappointments, we tend to find it hard to see the bigger picture. By not recognizing the spiritual elements in God's strategies in our lives, we miss opportunities to turn bad into good.

If we realize that eventually, Naomi became totally dependent on Ruth for almost everything, she must have counted herself fortunate that Ruth loved the Lord and was not going to be dissuaded to turn her back on Naomi. In this sense, without perhaps seriously considering it, Naomi was attempting to send away the person on whom she was later on going to depend for her own survival in Judah. When our vision is blinkered, and we become self-centered during our self-pity, we only end up shooting ourselves in the foot.

Christian churches and fellowships do what Naomi attempted to do on many occasions. Reflect on how many Orpahs that church leaders have returned back to their gods by their insensitivities and uncaring attitudes. How many drunken people, the homeless, and the drug addicts have we sent back to their "gods" because we have felt that they would spoil our good "reputation" or become a burden on us? Blinkered vision—that is what some of us disciple-makers sometimes have when things go wrong around us.

In Jesus' ministry, He encountered several such incidents, when people who wanted to follow Him were dissuaded from doing so for all sorts of reasons, even "good reasons". Bartimeus, the blind man wanted to follow Jesus and started shouting out for mercy. What did the people who were following Jesus do? Go back and hold Bartimeus by the hand and lead him to Jesus? No! Instead, the Bible says, the people told Bartimeus to keep quiet (Mk 10:48). Bartimeus was judged to be a time waster and a distraction and so was shouted down.

At another time, there was a believer who, for whatever reason, was not in the camp of Jesus' disciples. Despite not being part of the "camp", this isolated preacher started ministering in Jesus name. When the disciples of Jesus saw him ministering, they demanded that the man be banned. The disciples thought, "This loner was not accredited by us. So why should he be doing the same things that we the professionals do?" In their blinkered vision and narrow-mindedness, they wanted him to be stopped. Thank God for Jesus' answer. He said, "Do not stop him" (Mk 9:39).

Ruth

At another time, Jesus was busy teaching when a number of parents brought little children for him to bless. The disciples, thinking that this was an interruption of the profound teachings they were receiving from Jesus, turned round and started rebuking those who brought the children. Their vision was blinkered.

The disciples, like Naomi, failed to see that it was for these little children that Christ was going to die. The discipler's duty, like Naomi's, was to, as the KJV puts it, "suffer the little children" and not to frustrate or hinder their progress in the Lord. Naomi, in her understandable grief failed to see the bigger picture and instead tried to dissuade Ruth from following her into Bethlehem.

Paradoxically therefore, the first obstacle to Ruth's integration process was Naomi. Naomi was the most important person in the chain of Ruth's discipleship. Yet, she turned out to be an impediment. Her unwillingness to take Ruth on board, no matter her reasons, constituted the first barrier in the spiritual growth of Ruth.

For many immigrants, like Ruth, the first obstacle to their integration in their new environment usually comes from their closest neighbor or employer. It is the way the closest colleague at work, the person who receives the immigrant at the airport—it is how these persons receive and behave towards the immigrant that will determine the manner in which their integration will proceed in the strange land.

Similarly, it is how we care for and nourish our new believers that will determine their success in the future. It is when the first few contacts with newcomers make it their responsibility to be polite, warm and encouraging to the beginner that we can make their growth and integration in the fellowship firm and secure. Ruth did not have enough of that.

A Challenging Commitment

How should Ruth respond to such a situation whereby the one she wanted to follow was unwilling to fully help her? Should she give up because the first person was unwilling to take her under her wings, introduce and nurture her in the new environment? What should the immigrant believer do when the people he or she meets at the new church are cold and not welcoming? That was Ruth's first obstacle.

Ruth passed her first test by relying on her own deep spiritual resources (Ruth 1:16–17). Ruth's commitment stems from a deep love and commitment to Naomi's God. She wanted to go to Bethlehem because she had now come to believe in the God of Israel. Ruth wanted to worship Jehovah with God's people all the rest of her life. She was committed to Naomi because she was committed to Naomi's God.

Every Christian must operate by the same principle. He must recognize that all believers in the Lord Jesus Christ, regardless of their sex, race, color or denomination, are his own people. He should therefore stick with other believers no matter what. Commitment to the Church is crucial, just as much as commitment to the Lord Jesus. In addition to her love for God, Ruth also loved her mother-in-law. She wanted to stay with her long enough to prove this love to her. Her love was not in beautiful words. Her love was in her deeds. For Ruth, her love for Naomi amounted to sticking to her through thick and thin and in times of sorrow and joy.

This is exactly how God fashions disciples. It is when new believers are willing to commit themselves to the discipline and fellowship of the church that their love and calling would be strengthened and confirmed. So Hebrews encourages believers not to give up meeting together in fellowship (Heb 10:25). Some Christian immigrants disobey this instruction when they don't commit themselves to any church. That is not Ruth's way.

Having so harshly analyzed Naomi, we must now also acknowledge her immense contribution as a discipler of Ruth. Ruth would not have been so attracted to Naomi, her people and her God if Naomi had not displayed a life of godliness and dedication to Jehovah in front of Ruth. We can be certain that Ruth would not have so desperately wanted to follow Naomi into the strange land if what she saw in Naomi was a dull, unattractive, disinterested and hypocritical faith. Naomi after all did her homework well. She led an exemplary life in a foreign land. She, without doubt, must have been a holy mother-in-law for Ruth to have decided to stick with her.

Naomi is an example of the believer whose life is so powerful a magnet that people follow her even when she occasionally failed with her words. With such an example, Ruth could excuse her weakness and persist in following Naomi to Bethlehem.

Ruth

THE DEBATE ON THE INTEGRATION OF IMMIGRANTS

So how did Ruth's integration into the foreign land proceed? Since the recent spate of terrorist incidents in several countries, the question of the integration of immigrants has acquired prominent headline status. It is not uncommon to read in the daily newspapers about the problems of lack of integration of immigrants into the society. This lack of integration is blamed by some newspapers, government and civil leaders as one of the main factors in the increase in religious extremism and terrorism in general. It has therefore become very urgent for the issue to be addressed.

Unfortunately, identification of the problem seems to be the only point of agreement among policy makers and commentators. While every one seems to accept that something has gone wrong with the process of the integration of immigrants, it is not even unanimously agreed among experts as to what the meaning of integration is. To some people when they use the word integration, what they really mean is assimilation. By this they mean that the immigrant should reject their identities and cultural heritage and take on the new identity of their freshly adopted countries. Indeed, some countries pursue assimilation as an official policy even though they call it integration.

Such an approach to integration has however not worked where they have been pursued. Ultimately, assimilation impoverishes the culture of the receiving countries. One does not need to look far to see what the profound consequences of assimilation would be in most western countries. Supposing immigrants from India and China were to have abandoned all their wonderful cuisines, what a great loss this would have been to the Western menu!

More seriously, the major problem with assimilation is that there is no clear understanding of what particular culture an assimilating immigrant should adopt. It is obvious that recipient countries are themselves in a rapid state of change. Native citizens often have an uncertain understanding of what the country's culture and character is like. Hence to insist that immigrants should lose their identities and culture and adopt one that is not clearly defined is unlikely to be successful.

There are others who pursue the Multiculturalism model as the best means of achieving integration. What that means to them is that every immigrant is allowed to maintain and develop his or her own separate identity and culture. In so doing, the theory goes, the recipient culture is enriched.

This idea seems to be a reasonable compromise except that it has not worked in several countries where they have been actively pursued. In its place, many immigrants and their children have grown up without a sense of commitment and allegiance to the host country. It is clearly not in the interest of a receiving country to take in and shelter immigrants who in turn do not contribute to the sense of wellbeing and belonging of that nation. Multiculturalism as an integration model, especially when taken to its extremes, only seems to encourage clustering, lack of commitment and unity in the country.

A third approach is even more extreme. In the Exclusivist approach, immigrants are never integrated into the nation. Policies and laws are enacted to institutionalize and make it very difficult for immigrants to ever feel part of a nation. The aim here is clearly not to integrate, even though on many occasions, such governments do not plainly say this. They however enact laws and regulations which make it increasingly difficult for immigrants to become part of their new societies. At best, such people become second-class citizens who are unable to feel really part of the community into which they have moved.

Exclusivist integration policies have never really managed to integrate immigrants in countries where they have been either publicly or covertly pursued. They only produce immigrants who are segregated and isolated, and who do not contribute their positive energies to a country that sometimes badly needs them.

Against the background of this debate on what is the best means of integration of immigrants, an examination of the integration of Ruth into the Israelite society will teach us the Biblical Model of Integration.

RUTH, THE BIBLICAL MODEL OF INTEGRATION OF IMMIGRANTS

In this model, Ruth keeps her identity but uses it to fit into the jigsaw of God's programme for Israel. She never lost her identity as a woman and a Moabitess. However, Ruth contributed to the great nation of Israel and was duly recognized. When Matthew deliberately reminds us in Mat 1:5 that Ruth was a great ancestor of Jesus, what Matthew was saying was, "look how this foreigner was successfully integrated to become the ancestor of the Messiah".

Ruth's successful integration was a result of a combination of her own excellent personal qualities, the contribution of the community and God's grace. Obstacles were stack against her in Israel. She was firstly, a widowed woman. And in that society, that meant she was an outcast, and at the bottom of the pile. In addition, Ruth was a Moabitess. This was going to be a major obstacle to her integration. For, the Moabites had a bad history with the Israelites. They were descendants of the child that a drunk Lot had with his own daughter (Gen 19:37). This never earned the Moabites any good reputation with the Israelites.

To add insult to injury, it was the Moabite king Balak, together with the Midianites, who instigated the sexual orgies in the wilderness of Baal Peor (Num 25). Israel therefore never thought any highly of the morals of the Moabites. To have been a Moabitess was therefore going to be a major obstacle to Ruth's integration into Israel.

Despite these obstacles, we rather learn from the four chapters of Ruth that her Moabite origin was not a problem to her integration. Six times in the book, she is called "Ruth the Moabitess". This was clearly not meant to be derogatory, for she was highly respected by the people, who praised her devotion and love for Naomi (Ruth 4:15). In calling her Moabitess, the people were accepting Ruth as she was, as a person with another history, background and culture. What they recognized in addition however, was her faith and commitment to Israel's God. To this they were willing to respond positively (Ruth 2:12). Countries that are even nominally Christian can learn a lot from this about how to integrate Christian immigrants.

Ruth on the other hand, did not live in an enclave that was cut off from the Israelites. She did not exclude herself from the people, as if to emphasize that she was a foreigner who did not belong to the new country. In response to the recognition that the Israelites gave her as a Moabitess, Ruth voluntarily and out of love and commitment joined herself to the new nation and the new people. She overcame the obstacle of foreign identity, not through excluding herself and hiding away from the others but rather including and participating in the things of her new nation. What were responsible for Ruth's successful integration?

Woman of Substance

Ruth succeeded because she was a very hardworking woman. She was willing to work hard to look after her mother-in-law. She is the type of immigrant who never shies away from the meanest of tasks, grasps any opportunities that came his or her way and tries to make the best out of them. She was not averse to beg and ask for opportunities.

When, at the end of the harvest, Ruth heard that the poor and destitute people of Judah were allowed by the Jewish law to go into the fields and collect the leftovers, Ruth immediately sought permission from her mother-in-law to get some food for the family (Ruth 2:2). The foreman of the farm was so impressed by Ruth's hard work and professionalism that he publicly praised her (Ruth 2:7). Ruth's words to her mother-in-law in Ruth 3:5, summarizes her ethos and attitude to work. She said, "I will do whatever you say".

That is the kind of hardworking, "willing to do anything legal to survive" attitude that helps an immigrant to integrate into their new society. It was this also that earned Ruth her place in Israel's history. Without that attitude, without the hardworking commitment to make something great of themselves from the slightest opportunity, many immigrants will remain stuck in the poverty trap and excluded from the life of their new countries.

Also to her advantage was Ruth's way of speaking. This Moabitess was clearly very intelligent and knew what to say at the right time. We have already highlighted her first words when she committed herself to Naomi and Israel's God in Ruth 1:16–17. Notice also the skill and politeness with which she spoke to Boaz in the field (Ruth 2:10). With such manners in speech, it was not going to be long before Boaz would take more serious interest in her activities!

One of the major determinants of integration of immigrants into their new environment is their command of the host language. This is so basic to integration. Yet, unfortunately, many immigrants do not take it seriously. The absence of language proficiency and skills is the number one cause of the lack of good employment opportunities among immigrants.

When immigrants shut themselves out, and refuse to learn how to speak the local language, they will find it difficult to communicate with their employers, pass interviews, get promotion and lift themselves out of poverty. Immigrants deceive themselves by refusing to learn how to speak the basic language of their host countries.

Ruth

Supportive Network

The second major factor, which enabled Ruth's integration into her new environment, was the network of supportive people that she quickly found in Israel. Without the receiving country providing the atmosphere of welcome and friendly acceptance, the immigrant will not successfully integrate into their new environment.

Naomi, despite her initial protestations, was the first to hold Ruth under her wings, welcome her and introduce her into the new society. She was always there to support Ruth. When Ruth needed advice on how to comport herself on the field, it was to Naomi that she turned (Ruth 3).

Of course there was a mutual benefit to both of these women in their relationship. It was in Ruth's interest to stay close to Naomi and to be guided by the older woman in the integration process. On the other hand, it was also in Naomi's interest that she treated Ruth with respect and goodwill. For Ruth, after all, was the one who provided food and eventually a "name" for Naomi's husband.

The same principle applies to immigrants today. Host countries need always to acknowledge the contribution of immigrants and so continue to support them. When however, some countries treat immigrants as if they are a drain on their resources and refuse to acknowledge their role and input into the economic and cultural wellbeing of those countries, they are alienating the same people and hindering the integration of the new immigrants. Naomi must have certainly recognized that it was not in her interest to bite the hands that fed her.

Another source of support for Ruth was the women of Bethlehem. These women appear in this story as very lovely folks who never hesitate to comment on what they saw. They were there to welcome Naomi and attempted to help her to re-adjust to life back home (Ruth 1:19). They were also there at the christening ceremony.

Sociologists emphasize that one of the most important means of establishing, integrating and settling immigrants is the encouragement to voluntarily participate in the ceremonies, festivals and customary rituals in the new environment. These make them feel part of their new countries. The women of Bethlehem in their joyous and communal involvement acted as a strong support network for Naomi and Ruth and so enabled the successful integration of the Moabitess.

At her work, Ruth also found her fellow workers as important source of strength and support. The foreman was ready to acknowledge and praise Ruth's hard work (Ruth 2:7). That surely encouraged her. Employers play a fundamental role in helping immigrants settle. In companies and agencies where immigrants are treated with disdain, they soon become resentful and alienated from the society into which they have come.

When however, employers of migrant workers see to it that immigrants are treated fairly and with due respect then they will get the best from the workers. When employers ensure that immigrant workers have their appropriate orientation and job training enriched, then the immigrants, like Ruth, do contribute more than their best to the satisfaction of their employers.

Not only the foreman but also the fellow workers on the field were equally helpful and supportive of Ruth. Her whole experience on the field was one of calming assurance and people willing to help this stranger who had joined the nation. When countries look after the strangers in their midst, God blesses and enriches them. Jesus told his disciples that one of the heavenly standards that will be applied on the Judgment day would be our attitude towards strangers. (Mat 25:34–35). People and countries that obey Christ in this way will so be rewarded in His eternal presence.

One such person in the Book of Ruth, who behaves so impeccably and in obedience to this injunction was Boaz. Though clearly a rich executive, Boaz did not hesitate to publicly express his faith in God. When he arrived on the farm, notice the type of greetings that he uttered to his workers: "The LORD be with you" (Ruth 2:4). When he was first introduced to Ruth, he acknowledged and praised her for the sacrifice and commitment she had shown.

Boaz showed interest in the safety of the strange woman and ensured that she was well provided for. His integrity in response to the romantic schemes of Naomi and Ruth speaks volumes. Similarly, his open, transparent and fair manner by which he negotiated to marry Ruth at the city gate in Ruth 4 is exemplary. With such an employer and helper, why wouldn't Ruth integrate successfully?

Boaz knew and obeyed the several laws of Jehovah that enjoined His people to treat the stranger among them with love and kindness, and with fairness. Exodus 22: 21 for example reads, "Do not mistreat an alien or oppress him, for you were aliens in Egypt". Precisely because they were former immigrants, God reminded His people to treat all immigrants with respect. When nations forget, or worse, ignore the history of their ancestors, that they as a nation are descendants of immigrants; they soon resort to oppressing the new strangers among them. That was not how God wanted his people to behave.

By God's Grace

Ruth's successful integration was not just due to her own excellent qualities and the network of supportive hosts. She succeeded because of the grace and favor of God. She did her very best, worked hard, had the correct attitude, served her mother-in-law and employer and made every effort to fit into her new environment. Her receiving country also provided Ruth with the fertile ground to smoothen the process of this integration. Nevertheless, without the gracious acts of God at every turn of events, Ruth would still not have been successful as an immigrant in the strange land.

When the elders of Bethlehem pronounced their blessings on the marriage of Boaz to Ruth (Ruth 4:11–12), they were in effect recognizing this special grace of the God of Israel. He is the God who turns things upside down, not in the way human beings expect. This is why the elders compared this marriage with the infamous relationship between Tamar and Judah.

We discussed the story of Judah and Tamar when we were reflecting on the life of Joseph. There in Gen 38, we noted the strangeness of the story of prostitution, which resulted in Judah sleeping with his foreign daughter-in-law and producing an offspring. It was mentioned that the story, which superficially appears to be out of place, is indeed placed there in the middle of the Joseph story to give us a clue as to how to understand the whole theme of the life of Joseph. For, like many immigrant stories, it describes how God turns the evil experiences of those whom He favors for the good of His Kingdom.

The Judah and Tamar story, like the Ruth story, is an account of how, once again, God brings a "tainted" person into the lives of His people in order to fulfill His strategy. In this case God wanted a foreigner in the ancestry of the Messiah. This means that eventually, the Messiah is never a hundred percent Israelite. Instead, the Messiah, though springing from Israel, turns out also to be a descendant of an immigrant. That is what the story of Judah and Tamar was like. And Boaz and Ruth were continuing in that same biblical tradition.

In their blessings, the elders of Bethlehem perceived that when God admits foreigners who share the same faith as His people into the commonwealth of Israel, they bring some special blessings and fulfill His agenda in spectacular ways. The elders of Bethlehem therefore refused to be exclusivists. They did not resent and look down on Ruth. Instead, they yielded to God's active grace that was at work.

It takes God's powerful grace to shape our circumstances and work out our decisions to suit His loving purposes and so bless us on the way. It is when that ingredient is there, molding and fashioning out the details of our experiences that we will see success as immigrants. Ruth made a simple decision in following her mother-in-law into Judah. She loved her late husband, Mahlon. She loved Naomi and she loved Naomi's God. She therefore decided to be where the people she loved were. That was all. Yet, with God's grace on her life, a blessed result was guaranteed.

DISCUSSION QUESTIONS

1. Under what circumstances and situations do you think an immigrant should "return home"?
2. Which of the four models of integration mentioned in this chapter does your present country have?
3. Language proficiency is one of the most important contributory factors to successful integration. What do you think are the practical obstacles within your community, which retards how people learn the language of the country?

Jesus

The Word Became Flesh and Dwelt Among Us: God the Immigrant

THE PUBLIC DISCUSSIONS ON immigration, even among Christians, have not seriously reflected on a fundamental question. What was Jesus' attitude towards immigrants? Such a question should have been asked long ago, for during the time of Jesus, there were many immigrants of different colors and races in Palestine. Galilee in particular was typically made up of a mixed population. The Lord could not have avoided interacting with foreigners. Hence an examination of Jesus' attitude to immigrants is long overdue. Believers, who take the Lord's example as the norm of good behavior, will certainly appreciate such an examination.

Before such a question is answered however, a more basic question must precede it. Did Jesus' self-identity influence how He related to foreigners? This question is essential, because a person's self-understanding will influence how he relates to others. This is especially so with regard to foreigners. And Jesus is not an exception. It is after we have made some conclusions about how the Lord Jesus understood Himself, that we will be able to appreciate His attitude to immigrants.

Of course dealing with the question of Jesus' self-understanding is not an easy project. This is because, as Son of God, he is portrayed by the Bible in innumerably different ways. Jesus' personality is like a precious gem with many different facets, each one glistening with glory. God testified that Jesus is His Beloved Son (Matt 3:17) and Jesus Himself confirmed that He and His Father are One (Jn 10:30). His resurrection from the dead, according to Paul, was the final declaration by God that Jesus is His Son (Rom 1:4). He is also the Christ, the anointed One. This title combined several of the Jewish expectations of the coming Messiah—God's final prophet, king, Son of Man and servant of the Lord.

There are many other descriptions of the identity of Jesus in the Bible. 1 John 2:1 describes Jesus as our present "advocate" before the Father, who pleads on our behalf. Jesus is also the head of the church (Eph 1:22), the only Mediator (1 Tim 2:15) and the Shepherd and Bishop of our souls (1 Pet 2:25). He is the great high priest who intercedes on behalf of God's people. He brings, and at the same time, grants our supplications. Believers can therefore be sure that they have a "sure and perfect plea" before the throne of God above.

Jesus is the alpha and omega (Rev 1:8) and the great apostle who leads God's children in triumph (Heb 3:1). He is the author and finisher of our faith (Heb 12:2), the blessed and only potentate (1 Tim 6:15) and the captain of our salvation (Heb 2:10). Jesus is the chief shepherd (1 Pet 5:4), the faithful witness (Rev 1:5) and the forerunner and path-breaker ahead of us (Heb 6:20). He is the King of kings and Lord of lords (1 Tim 6:15), the Lord of glory (1 Cor 2:8), the Lamb of God (Jn 1:29) and the prince of life. There are many other descriptions of Jesus. These however illustrate the challenge—that we are trying to understand an unfathomable personality.

Despite these challenges, we need to focus on the type of description of Jesus' identity that would have been relevant to His encounter with immigrants. Our task in this chapter is therefore set out into two broad aims—defining Jesus' immigration status and describing His attitude to immigrants.

JESUS THE IMMIGRANT

It is not often emphasized that the Bible depicts Jesus as a stranger, an alien, foreigner and immigrant in the world. This picture in fact dominates the way the Gospel of John portrays the identity of Jesus. Somehow the earliest believers found the revelation of the "immigration status" of the God-Man Jesus to be very critical to their own identity and mission as His followers. This emphasis is desperately needed today.

John begins his gospel by describing the identity of Jesus as the Word of God. The Word, according to John, existed before the beginning of all things. He was one and equal with God and indeed, the same as God. It was only through His agency that the world was created (Jn

1:1–5). In the fullness of time, the Word became flesh, and made His dwelling among us (Jn 1:14).

The word, "dwelling" in John 1:14, is derived from the same Greek word that is used for the tabernacle of God in the Old Testament. John was therefore rightly pointing to the fact that, Jesus "tabernacled" in the world. In other words, Jesus Christ was truly the "tabernacle" of God among human beings. His physical dwelling on earth was as temporary as the tabernacle was with Israel in the wilderness. Just as the tabernacle symbolized the presence and power of God among His redeemed immigrant people in the Old Testament; so also was Jesus the temporary physical presence of God among His immigrant people in the New Testament.

Jesus' immigration status is shown by His self-awareness that He came from another place and was going back to this other place. His statement in Jn 16:28 summarizes this aspect of Jesus' immigration status. He said, "I came from the Father and entered the world; now I am leaving the world and going back to the Father". This indeed is the picture that dominates the portrayal of Jesus, the God-Man in the Gospel of John.

During part of His prayer in Jn 17:4–5, Jesus made a threefold emphases about His immigration status. He stated that in His other world, from where He came, He shared the same glory with the Father even before the human world was created. He then came into the human world to complete a task that the Father had set for Him. He came, more or less, as an ambassador of the Godhead, an alien of God's kingdom. In His prayer just before His death, the death that was to be the crown and glory of His mission, Jesus requests the Father to show forth His glory. Jesus was therefore conscious of His origin as otherworldly.

The origin of a person is the number one factor that determines their identity. Consequently, during ancient times people were named by their places of origin and who their kinsmen were. Even today, a person's basic identity is provided by the name, address, and place and date of birth. All these constitute the person's origin. Knowledge of the origin of the person defines who they are. For Jesus, His origin was from another world, and this consciousness heavily influenced His attitude in the world.

At another time, Jesus stressed the nature of the relationship He had with His Father in the other world from which He came. This, according to Him, qualified Him to reveal the Father to us. To Nicodemus, He emphasized that He is the only person who came from the Father's presence to the world (Jn 3:13). Jesus' origin qualified Him as the Person suited to reveal the Father to us. Simply put, and in the words of John, Jesus "came from God and was going back to God" (Jn 13:1).

This self-understanding also gave Jesus an urgent and unquenchable sense of His mission. He knew from the beginning that He was temporarily here on earth to fulfill this mission. He appreciated that it would be counterproductive to get embroiled in the things that had no significance to this mission. He told Nicodemus that He was sent not to condemn the world but to save it (Jn 3:17). He came so that He might complete the work of the Father (Jn 17:4). His mission was to bring the light into the dark world (Jn 12:46). This self-knowledge gave the Lord focus and energy in His mission.

Jesus' immigration status is important for the Christian's self-identity. It is when, as His followers, we appreciate that our true origin is not from the world in which we live, but that we are immigrants and aliens, temporary visitors on earth—that we will correctly focus on and pursue what our true mission in this world is. If Christians lose this self-consciousness, they will also lose their mission.

Not only did Jesus stress that He originated from another world, He also emphasized that He belonged to another world. Looking his opponents in the face, Jesus told them: "You are from below; I am from above. You are of this world; I am not of this world" (Jn 8:33). He could not have put it any clearer. Because He belonged to another world, His philosophy and ethos were also otherworldly. He lived by a set of principles that were fashioned after this other world. So for example, He told His disciples that He provides a different kind of peace that is unlike the peace that the world provides (Jn 14:27). Everything in Jesus' life was defined by the laws and principles of this "Other Place".

Jesus demanded that His disciples should have the same awareness of belonging to another world. He told them, "you do not belong to the world, but I have chosen you out of the world" (Jn 15:19). This perception of double personality is characteristic of all immigrants. It also applies to Christian discipleship. Their daily experiences, in which they were treated as different, were all testimony to the fact that the disciples of Jesus were citizens of another world. Living as a disciple of Christ requires us to imitate our Lord Jesus who lived as an immigrant in this world. He refused to value what the world cherished. He instead, laid down His life to serve His Father's purpose. And so must we.

Jesus

Jesus also stressed that He was returning to this other world, where He belonged and had come from. There, as He had promised, He is preparing a place for His people and will come back and take them to be with Him (Jn 14:1-6). Returning back to His Father's house therefore reminded Jesus of His mission and temporary immigration status on earth.

It may be argued that John's description of Jesus as an immigrant is metaphorical and does not necessarily make Jesus a "real" immigrant. Two responses will be given to this argument. First of all, the distinction between metaphor and "reality" in religious language is not as sharp as this argument assumes. Indeed the best ways that we can understand the nature of God is through metaphors. The Bible for example, describes God as Father, Shepherd, Judge, Refuge, Rock etc. All these are metaphorical. Yet, they also describe the reality of the nature and actions of God.

Similarly, statements like, "I have been washed in the blood of Jesus", or "I am born again" are both real and metaphorical. They are real in the sense that something radical has really happened to the person who makes such a profession. However, these statements are metaphorical because the experience does not in actual fact involve material blood or physical birth. It is a way of describing what has happened in spiritual reality.

It is the same when the Bible describes Jesus as an immigrant. The distinction between Jesus being a "real" or "metaphorical" immigrant is therefore not as sharp as is assumed. That God should even choose immigration as a metaphor for His presence on earth speaks volumes about the phenomenon.

Secondly, Jesus' life on earth was practically experienced as immigration. In his account of the genealogy of Jesus, Matthew carefully traced the ancestry of Jesus. It is therefore interesting that two of the prominent ancestors of Jesus that Matthew lists were immigrants. Tamar, who is named as Jesus' ancestor in Matt 1:3, was a Canaanite immigrant who dressed herself as a prostitute in order to have Judah's child. Ruth who fathered David's grandfather Obed (Matt 1:5), was a Moabite immigrant in Bethlehem. As we have discussed in the previous chapter, Ruth brought blessings to generations through her successful integration in Israel.

In addition, Solomon's mother, Bathsheba, was the ex-wife of Uriah (Matt 1:6), a Hittite immigrant who is also recorded in Jesus genealogy. Uriah the foreigner was one of only thirty-seven elite officers in David's army (2 Sam. 23:39). Therefore, though Bathsheba was Jewish, her previous marriage to the foreigner shows the influence of immigrants in the ancestry of the Messiah. Considering the fact that Matthew wrote his gospel with specific Jewish readers in mind, these deliberate references to foreign ancestors in Jesus' genealogy is remarkable.

In His life on earth, Jesus also experienced the immigrant condition when at a tender age, He and his parents sought asylum in Egypt. Indeed, Matthew understood the immense significance of this brief immigration as a way for Jesus to identify Himself with God's people (Matt 2:13–15). In paraphrasing Hosea 11:1 in Matt 2:15, the evangelist interpreted Jesus' movement to Egypt as a prophetic re-enactment of Israel's immigration to and from Egypt.

In other words, to Matthew, Jesus' immigration to Egypt was a way of declaring how God-on-earth associated with His immigrant people. Like Him, God's people are immigrants and foreigners in this world. The distinction that is made between Jesus' immigration status as a metaphor or as real is therefore quite artificial.

JESUS' ATTITUDE TO IMMIGRANTS

Bearing Jesus' self understanding as an immigrant in mind, we can now answer our first question. What was Jesus' attitude to the immigrants He encountered?

The gospels narrate several encounters between Jesus and immigrants. The unsurprising thing is that in almost all cases, the encounter with the immigrant was very positive. While a child, Jesus was visited by three wise men from the east (Matt 2). They came from far with precious gifts, knelt before Jesus and worshipped Him. At the same time as they were worshipping Him, the religious leaders were debating among themselves, and Herod proceeded to slaughter innocent babies to secure his throne.

Another foreigner who worshipped Christ was the Samaritan woman in John 4. Her faith and testimony indeed puts Jesus' disciples to shame. Then also is "the Royal official" of Capernaum who, unlike Jesus' countrymen, was willing to take the Lord's word at face value and believe without asking for signs (Jn 4: 43–54). Another group of foreigners, were the Greeks who sent a special delegation to meet Jesus (Jn 12:20). Once again, the Lord's attitude to them was positive.

Even the demoniac of Gerasenes (Mk 5:1–20) portrays a very positive response to Jesus. After being healed, he volunteered to be one of the inner circles of Jesus' company. When his request was refused, this foreigner, according to Mark, successfully spread the gospel in the "ten cities" of the region. His enthusiasm certainly surpassed those of the indigenous people who despised the Lord and cynically attributed His miracles to Beelzebub (Mk 3:22).

If one considers that the Jews regarded any contact with foreigners as a ritual defilement, then Jesus' deliberately positive attitude to immigrants was of revolutionary significance. By His positive attitude, Jesus was turning tables upside down. He subverted Jewish purity laws in order to welcome and befriend gentiles and foreigners. If Christians of today would allow the Bible to inform the ongoing international debate on immigration, Jesus' attitude to immigrants speaks loudly.

It may be useful to select three particular examples in the gospels where Jesus encountered immigrants for more detailed examination. We shall examine Jesus' encounter with people from the three common foreign groups in Palestine—the Roman Centurion, the Canaanite Syrophoenician woman and the Samaritans.

The Roman Centurion

The story of the Roman centurion from Capernaum in Matt 8:5–13 & Luke 7:1–10 is very instructive. We know that, since he had servants, he must have been well off. In addition, this army commander was also considerate to his servants, for he sought for healing on behalf of one of them.

Even more significant was the fact that this immigrant had a religious faith that was famous in the whole region! Luke indeed tells us that he was regarded by many as "worthy" of the blessings he was about to receive. This was because "he loves our nation and has built our synagogue" (Lk 7:5). Clearly, this immigrant had successfully integrated and excelled in His service to the nation.

When the centurion spoke to Jesus however, he did not emphasize his worthiness or special status as a renowned and benevolent philanthropist. Instead, his plea to Jesus demonstrates the depth of his knowledge of the ways of the God of Israel. He told Jesus, "I do not deserve to have you come under my roof ... say the word, and my servant will be healed. For I myself am a man under authority, with soldiers under me" (Lk 7:6–8).

In speaking like that, this man demonstrated that his theology surpassed that of his chaperones. While the Jews thought the centurion "deserved" to be blessed; the centurion on the other hand, thought he did not merit the blessings of God. He knew something about the grace of the God of Israel who does not bless people based on their eligibility, but based on His abundant grace. Being an immigrant, such knowledge was much less difficult for him than his chaperones.

The Roman centurion also demonstrates that he knew about another biblical immigrant soldier called Naaman, who received His blessings, only through the *word* of the servant of the Lord (2 Kings 5). The centurion's plea to Jesus was based on his knowledge of Naaman's experience. For, Naaman obeyed without seeing any ritual "performance" by Elisha. Like Naaman, the centurion believed that the word of God has more than enough power to touch and make a person whole.

The Roman centurion also knew about another foreigner in Jewish history called Jethro. Jethro may have been converted by Moses; or perhaps, he discipled Moses! Whichever was the case, when it came to the wisdom of delegation of spiritual authority, Jethro knew something that Moses did not know. As Ex 18:13–27 describes it, it was Jethro who taught Moses the principles of delegation of spiritual authority even before the man of God received the Ten Commandments.

The centurion interpreted his personal experience of delegation as a soldier in terms of the spiritual lessons that Jethro taught Moses. Just as Jethro discerned that Moses was "the people's representative before God" (Ex 18:19), the Roman centurion knew he was standing in front of a "Greater than Moses". Knowing such a history about God's past dealings with immigrants, the centurion believed in Jesus. He realized that in the general scheme of things, his foreignness made him a "nobody" in Israel. Yet, it was precisely this that drew Him closer in faith to Jesus.

Jesus commended this man's faith to be greater than any in Israel (Matt 8:10). Here, as on several occasions, Jesus used the faith and zeal of a foreigner to goad and challenge His own kinsmen to obey God (Matt 12:41–42). Like the centurion, Christian immigrants who live as ambassadors for Christ play an important role in the expansion of God's kingdom where He has placed them.

Jesus

The Syro-Phoenician Woman

The story of the Syro-Phoenician woman who met Jesus in the region of Tyre and Sidon (Matt 15:21–28 & Mk 7:24–30) is another example of how the immigrant's lack of social resources leads her to utter dependence and faith in Jesus. This Canaanite woman came to Jesus, "crying out" for help. She knew that those who cry out to the Lord in their distress will be heard (Ps 18:6). Yet, the obstacles that were stuck against her were many. As she pleaded, Matthew tells us that the disciples regarded her as a nuisance who was pestering Jesus unnecessarily (Mt 15:23).

When the woman could not be easily dismissed by such indifference, the next obstacle was the negative regulations against foreigners. Jesus quoted to her the common Jewish saying of His day—the official disclaimers and regulations about how Gentiles did not deserve God's blessings because they were outside the covenant. These were human regulations that insisted that it was only after the Jewish people, the indigenous people, the "locals", have had the blessings to their fill that the leftovers would be given to the outsiders, the foreigners.

Many of today's immigrants in various countries must have been told similar official statements on several occasions. They must have heard about how their immigration status disqualified them from any benefits. Some have been told that they could not be short-listed for jobs because they were foreigners. Many have heard that despite the fact that they may have the excellent CVs and the best experience, they will not get the promotion because they are foreigners. These official edicts that cut off immigrants and foreigners from sharing in the rights of taxpayers with the citizens are not new.

That was the sort of thing Jesus was quoting to the Syrophoenician woman. A modern paraphrase of what Jesus quoted to the Canaanite woman goes like this—"As you know, the law does not qualify you for this type of benefit. You are a taxpayer alright, but you are nevertheless disqualified from receiving these special privileges. You are way behind the queue. We have to serve the "locals" first, then the "EU" or "NATA" citizens, and then if there are some leftovers, you may have some".

The Syro-Phoenician woman would not be put off that easily by such official barriers. She didn't need the disclaimer read to her because they were operative in her daily experience already. She knew by her daily encounters that she was already at the back of the queue for the blessings of God. She knew that she was excluded and marginalized by the human laws designed for those purposes.

The Canaanite woman also knew that what she was asking from Jesus was not in short supply. She knew that because they come from the hands of the Almighty God, favors and mercies are never in short supply. There are more than enough of those blessings to spill over even for people at the back of the queue or outside it.

The Canaanite woman knew about one of her foreign ancestors in the Bible, a widow from her home country of Sidon, from the village of Zarephath (1 Kings 17:7–27). This widow of Zarephath, a foreigner, was the only person that the God of Israel marked out to feed Elijah during the prolonged famine (1 Kings 17:9). She was asked by Elijah, who was one of the "children", to use her final bit of flour to "*first* make a small cake of bread for me" (1 Kings 17:13; emphasis added).

After believing the word of God and obeying, the widow's blessings never dried up! This story about the widow of Zarephath was not lost on the Syrophoenician woman as she heard those common Jewish exclusivist regulations being quoted. She knew that God has always been in the business of overruling these exclusivist regulations. She also knew that the widow of Zerephath's son was revived from death by Elijah. And she also knew she was standing in front of a "Greater than Elijah". Why will Jesus turn her away?

Knowing these biblical facts about the non-exclusivist God of Israel, she could sweep aside the human edicts and commands that excluded her. "The people may exclude me", she must have said to herself, "but Israel's God does not exclude anyone". This is why she insisted that she must have her chance and her share of God's grace. Though despised and placed at the bottom of the pile, she also must benefit from the hands of Jehovah who gives over and above what people ask.

Many believers have misunderstood Jesus' statement, thinking that He was either being rude or at best not being helpful in pointing out the popular thinking of His countrymen. It should be remembered however, that in that culture, this type of "public verbal sparring or haggling", which anthropologists call *the Riposte*, was common. It was a natural means of assessing the seriousness of the woman's request. In the Riposte, speakers do not have to say what they personally believed. They just repeated the conventional way others may argue against another. The interlocutor's duty was to counter the public argument and show its faulty thinking.

Jesus

Accordingly, what Jesus was doing with His statement was to give the Syro-Phoenician woman the chance to show the faulty philosophy and application of Israel's purity laws that excluded immigrants and foreigners like her from the grace and favor of God. The woman, more or less, speaks for Jesus by showing that God never locks anyone out. Whether they are indigenous people or immigrants, and regardless of what the social and societal laws and traditions are designed to do, God welcomes all into His grace.

Like the centurion, the obstacle to the faith of the Syro-Phoenician woman merely acted as a stimulant and a motivation to perseverance. The arguments and rules against her only served as the inspiration to her believing even more. She would not accept that God would forever lock her out and refuse her a blessing. What kind of God would He then be?

The Good Samaritan

The Samaritans were closer in geography and history to the Jews than the Romans or the Canaanites. They were distant cousins of the Israelites, having descended also from Jacob. After the division of the whole nation of Israel into a northern and southern kingdom, the North established its own religious traditions and customs in competition with Jerusalem (1 Kings 16). This infamous history resulted in bitter hostilities between the Israelites and the Samaritans, as Jn 4:9 reminds us. A Samaritan in Israel was regarded as an apostate, a person whose soul was lost because of following other gods.

Jesus met several Samaritans in His ministry. The Samaritan woman in John 4 is one example. Whereas the Jerusalemites attempted to stone Him (Jn 10:31), and His own hometown of Nazareth tried to kill him by trying to throw Him down a cliff (Lk 4:29), a whole Samaritan city of Sychar on the other hand, professed faith in the Lord Jesus and begged Him to stay with them for two days (Jn 4:40).

It is therefore unsurprising that Jesus reminded the congregation gathered in the synagogue of Nazareth, that God singled out the widow in Zarephath and Naaman above Israelites for blessings (Lk 4:25–27). Somehow, these immigrants and strangers, these marginal people, tended to be more appreciative of the grace and blessings from God.

The story of the Good Samaritan in Luke 10:30–37 is illustrative of Jesus' positive attitude to foreigners. This parable describes how a foreigner so sensibly practiced his faith to the embarrassment of the religious professionals of those days. In using this foreigner as an example of practical faith and obedience to God, we learn something remarkable about Jesus' attitude to foreigners and the nature of Christian discipleship.

We are not told whether the Good Samaritan was living as an immigrant in Israel. The fact that the road on which the unfortunate victim was found was frequented by Jews, and that it was between Jerusalem and Jericho, suggests that the Good Samaritan might have at least been a temporary sojourner there. It is this stranger who, unlike the Levite or the priest, stopped to help the injured man by the roadside.

Of course, it is not explicitly stated whether the Samaritan acted in this way because of any particular religious beliefs he held. However, in highlighting his compassion on the injured man, Jesus implied that the Samaritan was obeying the command of God to love our neighbors as ourselves.

The Samaritan correctly interpreted God's Word regarding how to treat his neighbor. He was therefore as religious as the Levite and the priest—except that his religion consisted of a practical faith and obedience to God's Word. His religion was not in rituals and learning the correct clichés and jargons and exhibiting sanctimonious attitudes. On the contrary, his religion was in doing what the Lord commands. That is discipleship in its essence.

Reflect on how the Good Samaritan went about his ministry of loving his neighbor. Jesus said the Samaritan took pity on the victim, went to him and bandaged his wounds. He then put the man on his own donkey, and transported him to a hospital where he willingly paid the bill for the healthcare (Lk 10:33–34). What an amazingly practical example of discipleship to Christ through helping strangers and foreigners.

How Christians of today need to stop our self-absorption and self-importance that makes us discriminate against foreigners. Like this Good Samaritan, the Lord requires His disciples to come down from our spiritual high horses, and begin to bandage and help heal the wounds of broken humanity. That includes treating strangers with humility and kindness as our Lord did.

Jesus

DISCUSSION QUESTIONS

1. List as many different depictions of the identity of Jesus from the Bible as you can. For each one of the depictions, what do you think are the implications to how Christians should understand their own identity and mission?

2. Why is it that the portrayal of Jesus as an Immigrant, especially in the Gospel of John, has not been adequately emphasized in the churches?

3. What are the implications of Jesus' relationship and attitude to immigrants and foreigners to Christian Discipleship?

Paul, Barnabas, Stephen and Apollos

These People, Who Have Turned the World Upside Down, Have Come Here Also: Christianity was Largely Spread by Immigrants

WITHIN A MATTER OF months after the death and resurrection of the Lord Jesus, His small band of feeble and clueless followers, peasants and unschooled men and women, who hailed from the villages and countryside of Galilee, had expanded into hundreds of thousands of people and spread to all the cities and towns of the Mediterranean region. Within thirty years of His ascension, the gospel had spread to the corners and crannies of the Roman Empire. This very rapid growth of the early church to the uttermost edges of the Roman Empire within a few decades, in the absence of radio, television, internet and all the speedy means of communication that we take for granted today, is the most remarkable revolution that the world has ever seen.

The people of Thessalonica were absolutely right in their assessment of the influence of the Christian men and women who had recently entered their city. With palpable frankness and equally severe apprehension, they told the judge of the city, before whom a number of Christians had been charged—"These [people] who have turned the world upside down have come here also" (Acts 17:6). They were totally correct. The few believers were literally causing a revolution and turning the values and beliefs of the whole of the Roman Empire upside down. How can we account for the phenomenal growth of early Christianity? What were the secrets of such an achievement by the early church?

We have a medical doctor to thank for his meticulous investigation and detailed account of the spread of early Christianity. His record in the Acts of the Apostles provides us the clues for identifying the reasons behind this rapid revolution. Dr Luke was not just an interested historian. In his own words, he "carefully investigated everything from the beginning" (Luke 1:3). More than that, Luke was also an eyewitness of some of the events that he records in the Acts of the Apostles.

The Greek word that was used for eyewitness testimony is the same word that the English one, "autopsy" comes from. It is therefore appropriate that Dr Luke should provide us the "autopsy" of the spread of Christianity. He was not just a historian who was writing while removed by distance and time from the actual events. Luke was actually part and parcel of the events that he records. And he writes like a doctor who was surgically dissecting a human body to find the causes and effect of a disease. We can therefore expect that what he tells us in his account in Acts will give us the exact picture of the reasons for the rapid spread of early Christianity.

The first few chapters of Acts of the Apostle tell us that the major reasons for the rapid growth of Christianity were the resurrection appearances of Jesus (Acts 1:3), the events of the Day of Pentecost (Acts 2:1–41) and the fellowship of the believers (Acts 2:42–47 & 4:32–37). Also crucial were the speeches and miracles of the anointed Peter (Acts 2–3) and the persecution of the early believers (Acts 4:1–22, 5:17–41 etc).

After His resurrection, Jesus appeared, not only to his apostles, but at one time to more than five hundred believers (1 Cor 15:6). These appearances no doubt confirmed in the minds and hearts of the first believers that the Lord Jesus had conquered death. This surely strengthened their resolve to fulfill the great commission to evangelize the world. The outpouring of the Holy Spirit gave the impetus to their witness. The earliest Christians indeed received power to be Christ's witnesses when the Holy Spirit came upon them.

Since majority of the first believers were from the northern regions of Israel, especially from Galilee, the importance of fellowship and sharing of goods and property during the time while they were in Jerusalem was crucial for their sustenance. Those who were well-off among them were extremely generous and shared God's love with many of these poor and homeless people who had come to believe in Jesus. This practical and effective fellowship sustained the new church. As they sat, united at the feet of the apostles, they reflected on what they had seen and heard in the few months of Jesus' ministry.

Peter in particular had received a new sense of mission and courage inspired by the Holy Spirit. He became a new man with a passionate desire to show his love for His Lord whom he had betrayed but from whom he had received tremendous forgiveness. Peter led the new church with great zeal and power. His speeches and the miracles he performed confounded the understanding of the great theologians of his day. Luke records that these theologians "realized that [the believers] were unschooled, ordinary men" and were therefore astonished (Acts 4:13).

The religious leaders were so alarmed that they subjected these early Christians to harassment and intense persecution. This was perhaps out of envy for the success of these unprofessional and unaccredited preachers. It may also have been because of fear of a possibly violent reaction by the Roman government to the rapid revolution. Whatever the reason, the religious leaders unleashed severe persecution on the early church in an attempt to suppress its growth.

The harassment resulted in the illegal mob killing of one believer called Stephen. The death of this one man was enough to scare the many Christians who had congregated in the cozy fellowship of Jerusalem, into dispersing to other places and cities. Acts 8:1 tells us that a "great persecution broke out against the church" from that very day. Consequently, most of the members of this large congregation scattered throughout the countryside of Judea and Samaria.

The more profound result of Stephen's death however was on a certain Jewish rabbi called Saul. Luke tells us, that Saul was present at the assassination of Stephen and gave his approval to that illegal act. This event goaded Saul into a deeply personal reflection of what religion was all about. His first reaction was to fight against God's call on His life by threatening and harassing more believers. However, he couldn't continue to react like that forever. A few weeks later, while he was on his way to Damascus in pursuit of more believers, Saul met the Lord Jesus. On that very day, he was transformed by Christ into a new creature, the old passing away to give way to the new.

The rest of the story, as it is often said, is history! With his profound zeal and massive Jewish rabbinic intellect and of course the power of the Holy Spirit upon him, Saul, now turned Paul, led this rapid spread of Christianity to the uttermost parts of the Roman Empire within the next three decades.

The above summary of the swift and powerful growth of early Christianity is the usual account that many give as the gist of the story of the Acts of the Apostles. Though true, this summary has however missed

Paul, Barnabas, Stephen and Apollos

one major factor that Luke consistently refers to but whose actual significance has not been adequately emphasized. This missing but crucial ingredient is the phenomenon of immigration and the influence of Jewish Christian immigrants in the Diaspora.

Immigrants were necessary for the inauguration of the Church. We know this through the divine timing of the great events of Pentecost in Acts 2. One would have expected that after His resurrection and His several appearances to His disciples, Jesus would send them out to broadcast the good news. Jesus would have empowered them immediately with His Holy Spirit and send them out without delay. That was not what Jesus did however. Instead, Jesus specifically instructed His disciples not to go out on any mission yet, but to rather wait a little longer in Jerusalem.

During one of His resurrection appearances, He breathed His Spirit on them as a "down-payment" of what was going to happen (Jn 20:22). This was not the bona fide outpouring of the Spirit however. For, the Church had not yet been inaugurated. The disciples were hence commanded to remain still in Jerusalem and wait for a few more weeks before they could begin the mission. That main occasion, at which Jesus inaugurated His Church occurred five weeks after His resurrection, on the Day of Pentecost.

Why did Jesus ask His disciples to wait for those five weeks? Luke expertly explains the reason when he wrote in Acts 2:5–12

> Now *there were staying in Jerusalem God-fearing Jews from every nation under heaven* .... they asked: "Are not all these men who are speaking Galileans? Then how is it that each of us hears them in his own native language . . . residents of Mesopotamia, Judea and Cappadocia, Pontus and Asia . . . *visitors from Rome (both Jews and converts to Judaism* . . . we hear them declaring the wonders of God in our own tongues!" (Emphasis added).

The long list of aliens, visitors and strangers in Jerusalem basically means that the Day of Pentecost was also the day for immigrants. Simply put, Jesus asked His disciples to wait for five weeks because He wanted to inaugurate His Church on the day when immigrants had filled Jerusalem. His strategy required immigrants to be involved in the harvesting (Pentecost was the feast of harvesting). Immigrants were largely going to be the people who would spread the gospel. That is why Jesus chose that specific day to pour out His Holy Spirit upon the disciples. Until then, the disciples were strictly ordered to wait.

From Luke's record in Acts 2, there were three categories of immigrants who heavily influenced the spread of the early church. We may call them the temporary and permanent immigrants and the dispersed emigrants.

THE TEMPORARY IMMIGRANTS

The first group of people that Luke regarded as essential to be present and witness the events of the Day of Pentecost were the visitors to Jerusalem. These were tourists and sojourners to that great city. Many of these people were gentiles. But majority were Jews. For some, they were in Jerusalem on business. The big Jewish festivals were very important profit making events. Also present were the foreign tourists, philosophers and professional magicians who traveled to and fro in the Roman Empire to spread their ideas. Jerusalem at Pentecost was a great opportunity for their trade.

For others, Pentecost was the time to come and see friends and family. It was a major social event for the reunification of relatives and kinsmen. They brought goods and news about their progress in education and training elsewhere in the Roman Empire. Others returned to Jerusalem at Pentecost for religious reasons. The Jewish law enjoined all men to appear before the Lord in the temple of Jerusalem on pilgrimage, thrice a year. These were specifically during the feasts of Passover, Tabernacles and Pentecost (Ex 23:17).

These pilgrims came to the holy land to worship and affirm their faith in Jehovah. Many of them tended to be affluent, middle class and well educated. In addition, some were very devout Jewish believers. They took God's Word as seriously as they knew best and sought to worship Him with zeal and reverence. Coming to Jerusalem on pilgrimage, for these immigrants, was a very high point of their religious calendar. Jesus therefore wanted the disciples to wait for all these temporary immigrants to come to Jerusalem before He launched His church.

The Ethiopian Eunuch was a typical example of this category of immigrants who came to Jerusalem. We are not told whether he was there at the exact time that the extraordinary events occurred at Pentecost. His story in Acts 8 is however, an example of what God had started doing with visitors and pilgrims to Jerusalem at this time.

When he arrived in Jerusalem, the Eunuch must have at least heard about the miraculous work of Jesus and then by Peter and the rest of the apostles. He probably already knew of the prophecy about the coming Messiah, the servant of the Lord whose death would save Israel. Now, there were rumors and claims that this Messiah had come in the person of Jesus and more so, He had died a few weeks ago. His followers were now declaring that He is resurrected and still alive. On his way back from Jerusalem, the matter still bothered him. So he took his copy of the Scriptures and started reading to check the prophecy again.

Just then, God sent his servant Philip to the Ethiopian to preach the gospel for his redemption. Believing the word, the Ethiopian offered to be baptized there by the desert roadside. After his conversion, this most important foreign civil servant or minister went back to his country and no doubt influenced his countrymen to follow Christ.

We know this happened because the Church in Ethiopia was one of the most powerful churches in the second and third centuries, probably thanks to this temporary visitor to Jerusalem. There must have been many like this Eunuch. They came to Jerusalem as visitors, traders, tourists and pilgrims but went back to their countries as Christians. Imagine what happened when they went back after their visit to Jerusalem. That is one reason why Christianity spread that quickly.

THE DISPERSED EMIGRANTS

A second group that was instrumental to the rapid spread of Christianity was made up of people who moved in the opposite direction to the first one. Many of them witnessed the ministry, death and resurrection of Jesus. Now experiencing severe harassment and persecution, these eyewitnesses dispersed to other towns and cities to spread the gospel.

Luke makes it clear that the large number of believers in the first few weeks of Christianity was going to be difficult to keep together. Problems with looking after such a large congregation soon emerged, with complaints of racial discrimination by a section (Acts 6). It was understandable that within the first few weeks, the early believers should stay together and fellowship. They needed the Word of God very badly.

Jesus' ministry, as is emphasized in the Gospels, had wisely concentrated on the small group of faithful men and women who followed Him. When He had publicly taught and performed miracles, the response from the general population had not been extraordinary devotion as it was with His group of followers. His message, it is fair to say, was not as well known as His fame. It was now up to the disciples, the faithful eyewitnesses of all that Jesus did from the beginning (Acts 1:22), to teach the thousands who had come to believe in Him. Jesus had also taught them to make the remembrance of His death and resurrection, the centerpiece of their worship. All these needed to be established and consolidated, as Acts 2:41–44 tells us.

The ultimate purpose of Jesus' plan however, was not to establish a large megachurch in Jerusalem, with members cozily enjoying themselves under the powerful expository preaching ministry of the Apostle Peter. Jesus' plan was to spread the good news of the love of God to the whole world. Sitting still in Jerusalem was not the strategy. Hence, in God's wisdom, He allowed the intense persecution and suffering of these believers to lead to their emigration to the other regions outside Jerusalem. And as they went, in their zeal and passionate commitment, they kept on spreading the gospel.

Luke gives us a few examples of the exploits of these emigrants responsible for the spread of Christianity. Soon after the death of Stephen, Philip, one of the seven deacons, immigrated because of the persecution to the regions Samaria. There, and to the astonishment of the Jerusalemites, Philip performed miracles and preached the gospel with profound results. It was also on that mission that he encountered the Ethiopian Eunuch, resulting in the conversion of a very powerful national leader and potentially of a whole country.

Soon, Peter himself could not stay in Jerusalem. He set off on a mission, first, to confirm the Samaritans, and then to preach in the other parts of the countryside of the region. It was only as people moved out that the gospel spread. The fame of what had happened in Jerusalem was not enough to change people far removed from it. Those who saw and heard and experienced it, needed to go out and tell others about it. And this "going out", started as a result of the persecution that dispersed the large congregation. God will do anything to save the world, even if He has to make His own people uncomfortable and turn them into immigrants.

It is clear from the long list of people that Paul mentions at the end of his letters that some of these dispersed emigrants moved far off to the edges of the Roman Empire. In Rom 16:7 for example, Paul refers to two believers, who at the time of writing, were residing in Rome. He described his former fellow prisoners, Andronicus and Junias as "outstanding among the apostles, and they were in Christ before I was" (Rom 16:7).

Paul calls these Jewish relatives, "apostles" in the sense that they actually saw and heard the Lord Jesus in the flesh. Since Acts 1:21–22 defines an apostle as someone who saw the ministry of the Lord from the time of the beginning until His resurrection, Andronicus and Junias must therefore have been involved in the earliest periods of the Church even before the conversion of Paul. Since Paul did not start the Church in Rome, it is reasonable to assume that it was people like these who established the Church there.

Immigrant Christians from the earliest phase of Christianity, who were dispersed from Jerusalem to the uttermost parts of the world, established the church in Rome decades before Peter and Paul arrived there. It was because of the powerful witness of Christian immigrants such as Andronicus and Junias that a vibrant witness continued and eventually led to the transformation of the whole empire. When God wants to do something great in a nation, He often sends an immigrant. That was what happened.

THE PERMANENT IMMIGRANTS

A third group of immigrants were even more influential and necessary for the growth of the early church. These were permanent returnees to Jerusalem. They were Jewish immigrants who were either born-and-bred in the Diaspora, or went there as young people and were educated there. And they had then permanently immigrated back to Palestine. These returnees, who Luke describes as "Hellenistic Jews" (Acts 6:1) were largely responsible for the phenomenon of the rapid growth of early Christianity.

Again, in the wisdom and eternal strategy of God Almighty, Christianity was born at a most appropriate time in the history of the world. Just before the birth of Jesus, Alexander the Great had produced a very large but surprisingly stable empire. It stretched from Africa to as far as the borders of Russia today. He had dispersed throughout this empire, the various peoples and inhabitants to its other parts. These dispersed people included especially the Jews, who were by their history already used to the phenomenon of migration.

Thankfully, Alexander had allowed these immigrants to integrate successfully. They enjoyed immense peace and shared in the prosperity and wealth of his domain. When therefore the Romans eventually took over this empire, there were well-developed Jewish settlements all over the major nations and cities of the Diaspora. These Jewish communities were, in many ways, far more progressive and devout than their counterparts in Palestine.

Among these Jews, far removed away from the Holy Land, God stirred within them a massive desire and yearning to serve Him and return to Him by faith. Like their ancestors—Abraham, Isaac, Jacob, Joseph, Daniel, Ruth, Esther and so on, their love for Jehovah burned strong within them while removed from the Holy Land. Hence they began to look for a way of returning to serve their God while in exile.

Many of them interpreted their emigration from Palestine as a punishment for their sins. They knew that the Scriptures had warned about the consequences of rebellion against God while in the Promised Land. And on not a few occasions, God had indeed carried out the threats and punished them by banishing them to other lands (e.g. 2 Kings 24–25).

Knowing this, many of these immigrant Jews in Diaspora devoted themselves in repentance to seek after God and prepare for the return of the Messiah. There in the Diaspora, many begun to taste the grace and presence of God again, just as was experienced by Israel in the wilderness. The Hebrew Old Testament was translated into Greek in the Diaspora and there followed a serious study about what true religion was all about.

The excellent improvement in learning, philosophy and education during that era promoted rather than hindered this growth. Several immigrant Jews formed religious associations and revivalist movements to seek to restore their fellow countrymen back to God. Some decided to return to Palestine to help in this restoration and to prepare for the coming of the Messiah. For some, they returned in order to learn more about their religion. For others, they wanted to be exactly where the Messiah was going to arrive in Jerusalem.

Diaspora Jews who returned back to Palestine at the turn of the millennium, to all intents and purposes were more devout that some of their religious counterparts who had stayed behind. Unfortunately, many of those in Palestine had turned themselves into legalists and fraudulent religionists. To such people the work of God was not a matter of warm devotion and faithful obedience but the following of strict rituals.

Whereas many of the returnees took the Word of God more seriously; their counterparts, who had never been immigrants before, disregarded the weightier matters of it. Instead, they resorted to splitting of hairs and arguments about the minutest details of Scripture. It was in this circumstance that the "Hellenistic Jews", the returnee immigrants, permanently settled in Palestine.

Nehemiah, Ezra and Daniel

There are sufficient archaeological and historical evidence in the records of the various libraries of antiquity to support this summary of the religious movement among immigrant Jews just before the birth of Christ. We do not need to go outside the Bible however for our evidence. The stories of Nehemiah, Ezra and Daniel furnish us enough evidence to be extrapolated about the state of religious faith among immigrant Jews in the Roman Empire.

Nehemiah was a Jewish immigrant, who served as an administrator or its equivalent in the palace of the king of Persia four centuries before Christ. Like Joseph, he had successfully integrated and risen to a high position in a foreign land. There, in the Diaspora, we are told, Nehemiah heard about the poor state of disrepair of Jerusalem and its temple. He was clearly so upset that the king noticed that his performance had declined.

Nehemiah's intercessory prayer tells us enough about the state of religion among immigrant Jews (Neh 1:6-7). His desire to return and help rebuild Jerusalem parallels the general feeling among some Diaspora Jews during the first century. Like Nehemiah, many immigrant Jews of the first century returned to Jerusalem to try and put right what was going wrong with Judaism.

Ezra was a contemporary of Nehemiah. Unlike Nehemiah, he was a priest in exile and not an administrator. Together with Nehemiah, Ezra organized a band of up to five thousand immigrants concerned about the state of religion in the homeland to return and rebuild the nation. Ezra's efforts at reviving the people in Jerusalem to return to true worship, speaks volumes about how returnee immigrant Jews were more at the vanguard of leading the restoration of God's people back to Him. Ezra's zeal is repeated several times among returnee immigrants in Israel during the first century AD.

Daniel, who lived six centuries before Christ, was born in Jerusalem but exiled as an immigrant to Babylon. The captivity for him was, after all, not a bad thing. For this great prophet became a beacon of light in the dark corridors of Nebuchadnezzar's palace. His excellent education and training to become a noble civil servant in the Babylonian empire (Dan 1:4) would, in later centuries, be mirrored in the lives of many Jewish immigrants.

Unlike Ezra and Nehemiah, Daniel did not return to Jerusalem. His attitude and prayer in Dan 9 on the other hand, demonstrates again the nature of the faithfulness and zeal of God's people when they were outside the holy land. Many returnee immigrants who later converted to Christianity were as gifted and faithful as Daniel was. Like their earlier counterparts in the wilderness, the Jews, paradoxically had the best opportunities to experience the presence of God, when they were away from the homeland, in the wilderness of immigration.

These three biblical examples, though occurring centuries earlier, give us enough evidence of the state of mind and heart of the Jewish returnee immigrant. There is no reason to think that this changed during the first century. Returnee immigrants tended to be more in tune with God's Word and God's strategy for His people. Most were devout, zealous and hungry for God like Nehemiah, Ezra and Daniel. It is to this category of immigrants that Stephen, Barnabas, Apollos and Paul, men who turned the world upside down belonged.

THE IMMIGRANTS WHO TURNED THE WORLD UPSIDE DOWN

The Apostles of Jesus constituted the foundational pillars of Christianity. They saw all that Jesus did and were commissioned by Him after His resurrection to tell the story. Without them, we would not have had Christianity. Peter, as Jesus said, was the "rock" upon which the Church was going to be built. And important foundation stones indeed these men and women were. Their most important contribution was the *eyewitness testimony* that they have provided us. They saw Jesus, God-in-the-flesh, "close up". And they have given us an account of that experience. This is the foundation of Christianity, the gospel that the church preaches.

Peter, writing perhaps near the end of his life, accurately summarizes his importance by stating, "We *were eyewitnesses of his majesty*. For [Jesus] received honor and glory from God the Father when the voice came to him from the Majestic Glory . . . *We ourselves heard this voice* that came from heaven when *we were with him* on the sacred mountain" (2 Pet 1:16–18 emphasis added).

Paul, Barnabas, Stephen and Apollos

The importance of the male Apostles and the mighty women of God—Mary Magdalene, Salome, Mary the mother of Jesus, Mary of Bethany, her sister Martha and so on cannot therefore be exaggerated. This is why Jesus stressed the important ministry of the Holy Spirit in bringing to remembrance what He taught and what they witnesses (e.g. Jn 14:26).

These eyewitnesses told the story of how it all begun. And then when it became possible, their testimony was written so that thousands of years afterwards, we have the eyewitness account to feed our faith. It is therefore not right at all when some writers give the impression that Paul was the foundation of Christianity. Rather, Paul built upon the foundation of the gospel that was taught by Peter and the rest.

To Paul, Stephen, Barnabas, Apollos and many others of similar backgrounds however, are owed the credit for the tenacious and vibrant spread of Christianity to the Roman world. These are the people who took the gospel that the apostles taught and then spread it to the "uttermost parts" of the world. Each one of these people was also an immigrant. It is therefore important to examine whether their immigration status may have, in some way, contributed to their success and if so, how?

Paul the Apostle to the Gentiles

That Paul dominates the largest fraction of Luke's account of the spread of Christianity in the Acts of the Apostles is beyond question. Because a large portion of the New Testament is a product of Paul's letters, a significant proportion of Christian doctrine is inevitably from this man's ministry. This fact cannot be overstated.

The question to be answered however is this—Did Paul's immigration status in any way, influence his success? Did it affect his thought patterns, his character, his tenacity, and his devotion and faith? Could Paul's massive intelligence, his willingness to restart projects that failed all over again and not give up, and his flexibility have been due, in part, to his immigration status? Was Paul partly a product of an immigration experience that led to a man fit to be used as God's instrument of transformation and as His ambassador? From the records of Scripture, the answer that we find to all these questions is yes.

Paul was the purest of Jews that one may imagine. He testified that he was circumcised on the eighth day, and was "a Hebrew of Hebrews ... faultless" (Phil 3:5-6). He was however born, not in Palestine, but in the

Diaspora, specifically in Tarsus of Cilicia (Acts 22:3). Cilicia was a region in present day Turkey. The city of Tarsus was so progressive at the time of Paul's birth that the Romans who were in charge of it declared it as a "free city". This meant that the citizens of Tarsus were governed by the city's own laws and were not subject to Roman interference. That also made it "no ordinary city" (Acts 21:39).

Tarsians were well known for their intellectual and philosophical pursuits. Indeed, at a point in its history, Tarsus was regarded within the Roman Empire as higher in rank than important cultural centers such as Athens and Alexandria. Tarsus was also renowned for its textile and tent making industry—a profession in which Paul had some training. Perhaps, because his father acquired Roman citizenship, Paul was also a Roman citizen. This resulted in a rather potent cosmopolitan mixture of Roman, Greek and Jewish roots in Paul.

It was within such a sophisticated city that Paul grew up and was educated. We know he was significantly influenced by his education in Tarsus because when it suited him, Paul referred to that aspect of his history. So for example, when a Roman soldier was maltreating him, Paul reminded the soldier about his origins (Acts 21:39). At another time, when he was giving a lecture in the highly intellectual environment of the Aeropagus in Athens, Paul quoted one of the famous Cilician poets called Aratus (Acts 17:28) to buttress his point. His first-rate Greek classical education influenced him so that on two other occasions, Paul quoted other Greek poets[1]. Clearly, Paul had acquired his rigorous intellectual acumen, which made him one of Christianity's scholarly giants from his successful education as an immigrant in Tarsus.

Also in Tarsus was a very flourishing Jewish community who seriously studied the Scriptures. To quote the eminent Biblical scholar, Prof Martin Hengel, "The Jews in this area between the mother country and the Tarsus mountains were not only particularly numerous, as Josephus attests, but also very powerful and aware of themselves"[2]. Cilician synagogues were intensely involved in the study and analysis of the Greek Old Testament. This no doubt, had some profound effect on the young Saul.

---

1. Menander the Athenian comedian in 1 Cor 15:33 & Epimenides the Cretan poet in Titus 1:12.

2. Martin Hengel, *Paul, Between Damascus and Antioch: The Unknown Years* Westminster John Knox, 1997:158.

Several ancient books in which prominent Rabbis of those times refer to the Jewish people in Tarsus have also been discovered.

Moreover, we learn from Acts 6:9 that within the Jerusalem synagogues, there were devout Jews, mostly returnees and some from Paul's hometown region of Cilicia. They formed a "revivalist" organization called the Synagogue of Freedmen. These returnee immigrants in Jerusalem organized public debates about the faith. This illustrates the intellectual and spiritual pursuits of Paul's Cilician colleagues in Jerusalem.

Like many of his Jewish counterparts, it was when Paul came to Jerusalem, and studied at the feet of the Pharisee Rabbi called Gamaliel that his training and exposure to the culture and life in Diaspora lighted a fervent torch in Him. God was later on going to use all that fervency and intelligence for His own purposes and glory.

Subsequently, after his conversion and initial rejection by the brethren in Jerusalem, it was to Tarsus again that Paul went (Acts 9:30). It is not stated exactly what he did there, even though by agreeing to rejoin Barnabas back to Antioch and Jerusalem, it appears that Paul was most probably studying and reflecting on his newly found faith in the synagogues and libraries of Tarsus. He certainly was more prepared and made ready to serve God when he went to Antioch. Saul's life as an immigrant in Tarsus and his continued association with this background therefore adequately prepared him for the mission that he was to fulfill.

Barnabas the Disciple-Maker

Barnabas was the disciple-maker par excellence. He belongs to the category of Christians who do not make many headlines, but whose indefatigable commitment, friendliness and brotherly love strengthens and encourages other believers and turns them eventually into spiritual giants. Such believers are often not recognized and acknowledged in Churches. Without them however, most fellowships would ground to a halt devoid of any progress. Barnabas played that kind of disciple making role.

We first hear about him in Acts 4:36–37 where he is described as a Levite from Cyprus. He was nicknamed Barnabas (which means Son of Encouragement). He must have been relatively well-off because he sold a field he owned and brought the money to help the fellowship. The next time we hear about Barnabas is in Acts 9:27 where he literally held the hand of the rejected Paul and introduced him to the apostles. Unlike the other believers, Barnabas had enough trust and confidence in Paul. It was his nature to be trusting and encourage people who were different from him.

When the gospel begun to thrive in Antioch, outside Jerusalem and the apostles needed a disciple-maker and a confirmer of people to go and help the new believers, it was Barnabas that they sent (Acts 11:22–24). Later on, knowing the extraordinary gifts of Paul, Barnabas went to Tarsus to search for and recruit Paul into the ministry in Antioch (Acts 11:25–26). It was here in Antioch that the Holy Spirit set Barnabas and Paul apart for the Gentile missionary work. Barnabas remained the senior partner until they broke up over a serious disagreement (Acts 14–15).

The breakup of this partnership itself demonstrates the generous spirit of Barnabas. Paul felt disappointed with their young assistant called John Mark and so was unwilling to give him a second chance on their forthcoming and more dangerous missionary journey. Barnabas in characteristic manner on the other hand, could not relent and give up on the failed disciple. Unlike Paul, Barnabas correctly felt that John Mark should get another opportunity to undo his past error. Not able to agree, the two apostles parted company.

The result, thank God, was a "win-win" situation. Paul went further to other places and planted churches whereas Barnabas built up the young Mark who later wrote the first ever gospel bearing his name. Supposing Barnabas had also rejected Mark, we probably would not have had that vibrant gospel. Paul himself later reconciled to Mark and found him useful (2 Tim 4:11), and also patched up his relationship with Barnabas (1 Cor 9:6). The contribution of Barnabas to the spread of Christianity is therefore immeasurable.

Did the immigration status of Barnabas as a Jewish immigrant from Cyprus, in any way, contribute to his excellent disciple-building qualities? The answer, from the record of the Acts of the Apostles is a resounding yes. Luke was meticulous in informing us that despite his Levite background this early Christian giant was also an immigrant. We are told that he hailed from Cyprus. According to one of the Roman historians of antiquity, called Cicero, Cyprus, during the first and second centuries, was annexed with Cilicia. Barnabas most probably had similar first rate education and social background as Paul. They probably knew each other before their conversions. Like Paul, Barnabas was clearly an open minded, clever and cultured man. And that is why the intelligent proconsul of Paphos by the name of Sergius Paulus wanted to speak with him and Paul (Acts 13:7).

Paul, Barnabas, Stephen and Apollos

Similarly, it is more than likely that it was due to the fact that Barnabas was well traveled that the Apostles chose him first as their ambassador to Antioch. Because he had been exposed to the contrasting ideas and cultures of the different regions, Barnabas was open and trusting to other people's temperament. Such a quality does not come that easily to a person with a parochial life history. It comes more easily to a person who has been exposed to different cultures.

Stephen the First Christian Martyr

Few people are better known by their death rather than by their achievement in life. To Stephen however belongs the unique accolade of being the first Christian martyr. His story begins in Acts 6 as one of the seven deacons elected in the early church to help deal with the practical problems of caring for the needy within the congregation.

Despite the practical nature of his duties Stephen was soon not merely serving tables but passionately and intelligently preaching the gospel. In public debates, his opponents "could not stand up against his wisdom or the Spirit by whom he spoke" (Acts 6:10). Before long, they conspired against him, accused him of blasphemy, and brought him to the religious courts. When they could not counteract his highly charged and powerful defense of the faith, they, against due process, incited the mob that stoned Stephen to death.

Stephen's contribution to the rapid spread of Christianity was in two main areas. The first is in the manner of his death, which affected the young Saul and also led to the great dispersion. His manner of death acted as a massive goad on Saul's conscience and led to his conversion. It also led to the dispersion of the believers to several regions of the Roman Empire. Stephen's confident declaration just before his death that "I see . . . the Son of Man standing at the right hand of God" (Acts 7:56), and his repetition of some of the words of Jesus on the cross, must have reminded those who were present about the Lord Jesus.

In dying the way he did, this young man brought back the memory of the heinous offense at Calvary to the consciences of his murderers. That haunting picture does not leave one the same—not while God is pursuing them till they give in. Stephen's testimony at his death was therefore a major factor in the early spread of Christianity.

The second aspect of Stephen's contribution to the rapid spread of Christianity is in his insightful analysis of the meaning and significance of Israel's history. Stephen's rather long speech in Acts 7 can simply be summarized this way—"God appeared to Abraham not on the Holy Land but in Mesopotamia. He told Abraham that his descendants would be "strangers" in another land (Acts 7:6). Moses, who eventually delivered them from Egypt, grew up as an immigrant. That prepared him to lead God's people through the wilderness for forty years. It was also in the desert, that they had the tabernacle of God with them, the nearest sense in the Old Testament in which God lived with His people. In the wilderness, God was being an immigrant just as His people. Israel's forefathers had mostly sought after God when they were away and removed from the Holy Land. This God may therefore be worshipped by anyone and at any place that people would surrender to Him in faith".

Stephen was therefore, saying in his defense that even from the time of Abraham, God never boxed Himself to a place. Instead, God have been more truly worshipped when His people were immigrants away from the Holy Land. Jehovah is indeed a God of immigration. For, He cannot be restricted to a place or even by a single people. Stated another way, Stephen's long speech in Acts 7 is an extended legal version of the simple statement that Jesus made to the Samaritan woman—"God is Spirit, and his worshipers must worship in spirit and in truth" (Jn 4:24).

Of course such blunt words were very tough for the religious leaders to accept. Throughout their lives, they had thought that Jerusalem and its temple was the only place where they could truly worship God. Now however, having analyzed the Scriptures, Stephen tells them that in actual fact, all through the history of Israel, God has been acceptably worshipped, probably in an even more genuine sense, outside Jerusalem. This was a very revolutionary understanding of the Old Testament to Jewish ears. The religious leaders couldn't accept this interpretation and so proceeded in their anger to kill Stephen.

There is no doubt that Stephen's powerful message, that the God of Israel has always been the God of all the earth and hence men and women can tangibly experience Him regardless of where they were, had a tremendous effect on the early Christians. The earliest believers begun to ask themselves—"if God dealt with our ancestors in so close a manner in foreign and distant lands just as He did with this Holy Land, why then are we sitting here in Jerusalem?

If God has been and will be real to us outside of Jerusalem, in the far away places as He did with Abraham, Joseph, Moses, Nehemiah, and Daniel why should we restrict Him to the Holy Land? And if God is to be worshipped everywhere and anywhere in Spirit and in truth, why are we His ambassadors, sitting here in Jerusalem?"

From then on the early Christians had no particular qualms about being uprooted to other places to spread God's word. They knew that they were merely following the traditions of the God who uses immigration as the vehicle to spread His Kingdom. Though Stephen died in his prime, his words, while condemned as blasphemous by the religious experts, have powerfully influenced the thinking and attitude of Christianity forever. That inspiring speech in defense of the gospel was his lasting contribution. After Stephen, the temple in Jerusalem, the city itself and the Holy Land, served only as the founding station but not the nerve center of Christianity.

And it is remarkable to note that, centuries later, a similar situation happened. The Church of Christ attempted in the middle ages to cage God into one place, and insisted that only a particular type of person or language or only the pope ruling from Rome was qualified to interpret the Word of God. At the time, another intelligent young man by the name of Martin Luther followed "the Stephen way" and produced a thesis that shook Christianity back to what it ought to be. Luther's effect was only a smaller scale of Stephen's.

Need we ask whether such a contribution by Stephen was made possible because of his immigration status? His Greek name alone suggests that, at least, he was a descendant of Jewish immigrants. He certainly operated among the group of Jewish returnees in the "Synagogue of Freedmen" (Acts 6:9). In addition, his speech typically employs the Greek translation of the Old Testament which was the popular version used by immigrant Jews in Jerusalem.

Moreover, it is obvious that only a person who was used to life that did not depend on the temple and on Jerusalem would have been so much as bold as Stephen to preach the sermon he did. The words of Stephen could only have come from a Jewish immigrant who had seen God at work elsewhere outside Jerusalem. He must have reflected on and studied the Scriptures in relation to the subject for sometime. When God wanted to change the world, he sent Stephen, an immigrant, to preach that sermon.

Immigrants of the Kingdom of God

Apollos the Eloquent Preacher

The contribution of the young Jewish immigrant from Alexandria of Egypt to the rapid spread of early Christianity is not as much as those of Paul, Barnabas or Stephen. His importance lies mainly in the influence he exerted in two vital first century churches—at Ephesus and Corinth. We cite him only to highlight how immigrants such as Apollos were used by God to advance his kingdom.

We first hear about him in Acts 18:24–26 where it is stated that though an intelligent man, he had some inadequacies in his theology. He was duly taken under the wings of the influential Pauline couple by the name of Aquila and Priscilla and "taught about Jesus more accurately". The discipleship process was so successful that Apollos was sent to Corinth in Achaia to build up the church there. His ministry in Corinth so flourished that some believers preferred him to the apostles Paul and Peter (1 Cor 3:4–6). He must have been very good to have been compared with Paul and Peter.

The knowledge, passion and eloquence of Apollos and the tremendous effect he had in these churches will not surprise anyone who knows the history of the Jewish immigrants in Alexandria during the first century. Established as one of Alexander the Great's most important cultural bases in his Empire, this Egyptian city was one of the key cities in the world of that period. Attending a university in Alexandria is akin to attending Harvard, Yale, Oxford or Cambridge today.

More importantly the Jewish community in Alexandria was the most advanced and religious of the time. It was in Alexandria that the Jewish teacher and philosopher called Philo lived and taught. So it is no wonder that Apollos should possess similar qualities. It was such a person and many more like him who planted, watered and harvested the growth of the early church. Immigrants like these in the Lord's hand turn cities and countries they enter upside down for Christ the King. Christians who truly live as disciples of Christ change their environments without recognition.

DISCUSSION QUESTIONS

1. In what practical ways can a congregation help new immigrants in their area?
2. What are the possible dangers to believers regarding themselves as aliens and immigrants in the world?
3. How would you summarize the message of this book?

Final Thoughts

Immigration and the Future of Christianity in the West

IT IS UNDENIABLE THAT the Bible's records on the positive influence of immigration on religion are impressive. The obvious question that must be addressed is what the implications are to the ongoing international debate on immigration? What are we to make of the vast biblical data on immigration that have been analyzed in the preceding chapters?

My concern, throughout the preceding pages, has been to restrict the reflections to Christian immigrants. In particular, I have in mind the effect of immigration on the future of Christianity in the West. Hence the application question needs to be more focused in this way: In the present dismal situation of Christianity in the West, particularly in Europe, is there a positive role to be played by Christian immigrants to stem the downward spiral?

Of all the lessons highlighted in the series of preceding reflections, three immediately answer the above question. And these are of relevance to individual Christian immigrants, Churches and nations. To the individual Christian immigrant, the lessons of these reflections imply that they have been placed where they are for a particular mission and strategy to do with the plan of God. All Christians, wherever in the world that they are, must live in such a way that they fit into God's unfailing plan to redeem the world. However, this is even more pertinent for the person who has, for whatever reasons, been displaced to another land.

To such a person, with the powerful combination of exposures to different cultures, experiences, personalities and outlooks, belongs the responsibility and opportunity to see the work of God in fresh ways. Such people are best placed to bring His kingdom into their corner of the world where God has displaced them to. If such a person has been reading these reflections, then the call to him or her is to a life of renewed commitment to the Lord's commands. Christian immigrants are where they are now to spread God's Word. They should resolve to remain firm and not be discouraged. Instead they need to draw on the spiritual resources God is making available for their growth and mission as Christ's ambassadors, as immigrants of the kingdom of God.

The significance of these reflections also holds true for every other Christian. Since all believers are immigrants and resident aliens in this world, the challenge to be ambassadors of Christ goes to all believers. We must all live in such a way that our faith and commitment would show forth the glory of Christ the King. The call to live as immigrants therefore goes out to every believer. No one can escape the command of the Lord that we spread His fragrance wherever He has placed us.

To the Church of Christ, the significance of the words of this book is equally vital. A church that has lost its identity will soon lose its mission. When we become indistinguishable from the world, we cannot change it. When we enter into competition with unbelievers, adopt their values and strategies we will fail to impress them with the gospel. If we cease to be light and salt of our society; that society, along with us, will have no future.

Jesus calls His Church back to where He wants it to be. He wants us to think, behave and live like strangers and immigrants. He wants us to influence the sinking world in such a way that we can at least save some. If we want our fellowship members to be true disciples of the Lord Jesus Christ, then we should put on the cloak of immigrants and live as such.

This also requires us to welcome the new ideas, passion, and commitment of Christian immigrants. Though displaced because of all sorts of reasons, they are nevertheless instruments and ambassadors of God's transformation. They bring to the Church of Christ, some freshness, passion and new insights that we neglect to our own peril.

To countries that are blessed to be recipients of Christian immigrants, the implication of the lessons of this book is also significant. Christian immigrants have come as the ambassadors of blessings, as Christ's change agents. They bring to the new countries a new blessing through the work of the Holy Spirit. Welcome them.

This is not to argue for open unlimited admission of all Christian immigrants into countries. The borders of countries have important

Final Thoughts

significance in the maintenance of peace and tranquility in the world. Governments have divinely required responsibilities to protect its citizens against fraudulent and maliciously minded foreigners. This alone requires them to sensibly control immigration.

Yet, a blanket approach at suspecting any foreigner as having malicious intentions is an over-reaction to such responsibilities. An antagonistic attitude to all immigrants, regardless of their religion and belief only results in a state of affairs not unlike what Jesus found among his own countrymen. Discernment is clearly called for in the present international debate on immigration.

God was not being in anyway illogical when He told Israel that though He does not show partiality and accepts no bribes, He defends the cause of the needy orphan and widow. For some reasons, God "*loves the alien*". He therefore commanded Israel, "*You are to love those who are aliens*, for you yourselves were aliens in Egypt" (Deut 10:17–19). Countries who obey God in this way are blessed.

www.ingramcontent.com/pod-product-compliance
Lightning Source LLC
Chambersburg PA
CBHW070928160426
43193CB00011B/1616